NO OUTCASTS

NO OUTCASTS

*the public witness of
Edmond L. Browning
XXIVth Presiding Bishop of
The Episcopal Church*

Narrated and edited by
Brian J. Grieves

Forward Movement Publications
Cincinnati, Ohio

Photographs:

Front cover
Color – Episcopal News Service photo
by James Thrall
Black and white – David A. Werth

Back cover
Top – Morgan photo
Bottom – Patricia Aboussie

Page 3
Episcopal News Service photo

Published by
Forward Movement Publications
412 Sycamore Street, Cincinnati, Ohio 45202

DEDICATION

This compendium is dedicated to my many colleagues who served on the staff of the 24th Presiding Bishop at the Episcopal Church Center and its field offices. Many of them will remember in these pages their roles assisting Bishop Browning in his public witness. They deserve much respect and recognition for their competence and many accomplishments.

I also dedicate this work to Dr. Pamela Chinnis, president of the House of Deputies, whose own public witness demonstrated courage and sensitivity during often difficult and turbulent days; and finally to Edmond and Patti Browning for the faithful witness they have left for the whole church.

ACKNOWLEDGMENTS

I want to thank those colleagues who took the time to cull their files and provide material for this publication and to those who read drafts and provided helpful suggestions, and particularly Irina Ottley, my valued secretary, who spent many hours retrieving much needed information, and Ruth Anne Garcia, who helped with the initial gathering of material, and to James Solheim, James Thrall and Jack Donovan for their help in providing materials and photos.

And I owe a special debt to Charles Long, whose wise counsel and editing experience was indispensable in completing this project.

The Rev. Canon Brian J. Grieves
Director, Peace and Justice Ministries,
The Episcopal Church

TABLE OF CONTENTS

Dedication 4
Acknowledgments 4
Table of Contents 5
Introduction 7

I – PRINCIPLES
Diversity, Inclusivity and Unity 13
Context for a Public Witness 21
Church/State Relations 38

II – ISSUES
Justice, Peace and the Integrity of Creation 45
Coal Miners 57
Gun Control 60
Gambling 63
Children 65
Capital Punishment 69
Women's Issues 71
Abortion 82
Human Sexuality 88
AIDS 105
Racism 111
American Indians 123

III – PLACES
South Africa 131
Africa 143
The Middle East—Search for a Lasting Peace 145
    Gulf War 161

Central America and Panama 174
    El Salvador...174
    Nicaragua..179
    Panama..184
The Caribbean...187
    Haiti—The Overthrow of Aristide 187
    Cuba...190
Asia...192
    China..192
    The Philippines 194
    Japan 200
    Burma 201
Europe...203
    Bosnia-Herzegovina 203
    Ireland 208
    Russia...208
The Pacific 211
    Hawaii 211

IV – PEACEMAKING

Nuclear Weapons 213
War..215

INTRODUCTION

Edmond Lee Browning was elected 24th Presiding Bishop of the Episcopal Church on September 10, 1985, in Anaheim, California. He had been a bishop since his election as bishop of Okinawa in 1967. He later served as bishop in charge of the American Convocation of Churches in Europe and for two years as head of World Mission for the national church until his election as bishop of Hawaii in 1976. He was in his ninth year in Hawaii when elected Presiding Bishop.

The breadth of his experience from Asia to Europe to his post at World Mission and finally back to the Pacific gave him as broad a preparation for the position of Presiding Bishop as any of his 23 predecessors.

He is a native Texan, born in Corpus Christi, March 11, 1929. A lifelong Episcopalian, he was nurtured in part for the ordained ministry by his experiences at Camp Capers, a diocesan camp. He attended seminary at Sewanee during that school's most tempestuous period in the early days of the civil rights movement. His stance as a young student in favor of integrating this southern school in the heart of segregated America was a sign of the kind of prophet he would become.

It was during his Sewanee days that he met Patricia Sparks on a blind date while home on Christmas vacation. She was later to become his wife, known to all affectionately as Patti. They had five children who grew up to pursue five distinctive professions: lawyer, architect, physician, priest and tennis coach. Browning and Patti always modeled a team ministry and made sure to include spouses whenever possible.

After serving two congregations in West Texas, Browning was appointed a missionary to the Church in Japan in 1959. He was eventually assigned to a congregation in Okinawa until his election as bishop in 1967.

He was generally beloved in places where he served in his ministry, and gained the respect of those who differed with him through his patience and willingness to listen. He was regarded as a pastor who never feared to exercise prophecy. While bishop of Europe, he advocated amnesty on behalf of "draft dodgers" who fled to Europe during the Vietnam War. Later, when he was in New York as head of World Mission, the White House called to tell him the President had declared amnesty.

In Hawaii, Browning, serving in a diocese with a large military community, became outspoken in his criticism of the nuclear arms race, declaring in the voice of the Lambeth Conference that nuclear weapons were incompatible with the gospel of Jesus Christ. But as pastor, he reminded his diocese that he was bishop to the whole flock of Christ and that included military families. His quarrel was not with them, but with government policy.

While some tagged him as a liberal, he shunned labels and rooted himself in an incarnational theology. When he was elected Presiding Bishop, he was well known to his episcopal colleagues, and was acknowledged as a mature member of the house of bishops, well liked and accessible.

During his time as Presiding Bishop, people meeting him for the first time were often disarmed by his easy and comfortable manner. There was no pretense about him and he always enjoyed a good story and a laugh, as did Patti. He was a sports enthusiast who always kept box seats for Yankee games, most of which he gave away to staff. He lightly referred to this as a ministry and was overjoyed when the Yankees won the 1996 World Series.

The Brownings had other interests which revealed something of their character. Patti rarely passed a homeless person on the streets of New York without offering some money. She and the Presiding Bishop adopted one particular man whom they encouraged into a substance abuse program. They also sought a housing placement for him.

Patti never missed the daily Eucharist at the Church Center chapel when she was in New York, although she would admit to being late from time to time. She had a strong prayer life and prayed for her husband and the staff every day. In a very quiet way Patti was a strong spiritual presence at church headquarters.

Despite his incredible schedule, the Presiding Bishop found time for occasional retreats to his Pennsylvania cabin which he dearly loved. Living in the apartment above the national offices never let him feel "off duty" and he and Patti relished their few times at the cabin, which Patti affectionately called Dogpatch.

The demands of his office were enormous and his travel schedule kept him on the road about 70 percent of the time. Although his tenure began with a chief of staff, a consultant advised him to do without one which he did until late in his term. While many good things happened in those years, he later regretted not having such a person throughout his term, particularly after he discovered that the treasurer had embezzled the church out of $2.2 million. This was a devastating experience, especially since the treasurer was a woman and he had made such a great commitment to filling important posts with women and people of color. Despite that betrayal, he showed his tenacity by setting the church's fiscal house in order before the end of his term.

Role of the Presiding Bishop

Throughout his years as Presiding Bishop, he recognized the prophetic role of his office as being one of his primary duties.

He understood that only the Presiding Bishop could speak for the whole church between sessions of the General Convention (every three years) and Executive Council (three times a year). He carried the mantle of leader and many active church members expected and wanted to hear from him. He was also Primate, meaning that in his office and person he represented the

Episcopal Church to Anglican partners worldwide. In this role he both heard and gave voice to Anglican partners and expressed Episcopal Church views.

He dutifully articulated church policies of Convention and Council. He was also unafraid to address issues which were not clearly stated in policy, as in his opposition to the Gulf War and his response to the Los Angeles riots in 1992.

A woman wrote to him early in his term, incensed at a recent position he had taken. She asked him by what authority he could speak for all Episcopalians. In a friendly reply he said he could not speak for any individual Episcopalian but would speak in his own voice and for the policies of the church whenever and wherever his conscience dictated.

Browning felt a special obligation to address himself to the three American Presidents who served while he was Presiding Bishop. Each relationship was different.

Ronald Reagan shut out the mainline religious leaders. It was a dark time for denominational offices in Washington, who were ignored by the Reagan White House in favor of leaders from the religious right.

But Browning did have his day with President Reagan. That was Easter day, 1984, when Reagan attended St. Andrew's Cathedral, Honolulu, while Browning was bishop. During his sermon, Bishop Browning referred to the President's visit as a blessing, and preached a generally positive Easter message. But the media picked up a short phrase in which Browning criticized the government for turning its back on the poor. The story ran in papers all over the country and the Boston Globe referred to Browning as Tip O'Neil in a cope. The angry letters that Browning received were perhaps preparation for his years as Presiding Bishop.

President Bush was usually accessible to Browning, agreeing to a courtesy call early in his administration. Bush, a fellow Episcopalian, and Browning found themselves at odds on numerous occasions, most notably during the lead-up to the Gulf War. But Browning also found occasion to praise Bush, as when the President stood up to the Israeli lobby and refused to approve loan guarantees until settlement building ceased in the occupied territories. Of the three Presidents during Browning's term, Bush was the most readily accessible to Browning personally.

President Clinton also made himself available to mainline religious leaders and Browning received several invitations to the White House. He joined religious leaders in a meeting shortly after the inauguration in 1993 and again at an intimate breakfast meeting to discuss civility in public life in August, 1994. Browning supported some administration policies and opposed others. On Iraq, he expressed opposition to sanctions after the Gulf War. He also castigated the US veto at the UN which implied US recognition of Israel's annexation of East Jerusalem. And Browning called the White House to express his displeasure at Clinton's support for the welfare reform legislation of 1996. Browning supported Clinton when his views matched those of the church, as in Clinton's support for affirmative action and health care reform.

One of Browning's accomplishments was expansion of the role of the Episcopal Church's Washington Office during the course of his term assuring that the Episcopal Church's positions, as determined by General Convention and Executive Council resolutions, were regularly and effectively communicated to the various branches of government. He himself made several visits to the Congress where he made friends on both sides of the aisle. He visited the State Department as well as the White House and also called on General Colin Powell, an Episcopalian, then head of the Joint Chiefs of Staff.

This publication does not include everything that Browning

said during his term in office, but it does provide broad exposure to many of his views. What follows is a testimony to the various ways Edmond L. Browning took seriously his charge to be a prophetic voice in the latter years of the 20th century.

I
PRINCIPLES

DIVERSITY, INCLUSIVITY AND UNITY

"There will be no outcasts." There is no way that Bishop Browning could have known when he uttered those words in Anaheim in 1985 two days after his election as Presiding Bishop that they would stay with him as a central theme throughout his term. Nor could he have known how heartening those words would be to some and how threatening to others. As the years went by, he found himself returning repeatedly to this theme.

Acceptance speech, General Convention, September 12, 1985

I have today invited you, all of you, to share the diversity of views, of hopes, of expectations for the mission of this Church. I want to be very clear—this Church of ours is open to all—there will be no outcasts—the conviction and the hopes of all will be honored.

Address to House of Bishops, San Antonio, September 22, 1986

There is no more important role for this Office than to affirm the tremendous diversity of this Church of ours, and at the same time hold the diversity in the unity of mission and servanthood . . .

I am certain that it comes as no surprise that there are some anxious moments in this job you have given me—certainly one of them is how to enable the diversity to sense its unity in open mission. I have been helped to understand over eight months that it's not only possible but will happen when, in the midst of our diversity, the focus is constantly on the centrality of the Lordship of Christ and his servanthood ministry . . .

I realize there are many risks involved in inclusiveness. There is the risk of losing identity and cohesiveness. There is the risk of vagueness. I believe that these are the risks the Anglican Communion has always taken, and it is what has made it great. Indeed, the Anglican Church is at its best when it holds together the tension of diversity—a Cranmer and Laud, a Hooker and Temple, a Hines and an Allin.

When Anglicanism lost its tolerance for tolerance, it no longer served the Lord. But when it had a high sense of tolerance, an openness, an inclusiveness, it found its greatness. Anglicanism has a high tolerance for ambiguity—it is a gift we give to our religious partners. It is a gift from God we need to accept and exercise. It means taking risks, facing pain and tension, living with seeming contradictions. With God's grace, we will accept and exercise this ministry of inclusiveness, holding together the many parts of Christ's Body, bringing meaning to the lives of all God's children out of our deep spirituality.

In *unity* and *diversity*, we gather to answer the call of Christ Jesus, who is the source of our strength and the focus of unity.

Remarks to Staff, February 1987

This past year has brought me more than just information gathered in a passive listening process—it has engaged me in a deep existential spiritual exercise. Yes, I sat at dozens of meetings, but I also stood in many places of pain. I stood with the Archbishop of Canterbury and Archbishop Tutu at the Crossroads Settlement outside of Cape Town. I stood with Bishop Kafity of Jerusalem and the Middle East in refugee camps in the Gaza. I had lunch with the homeless in Atlanta. I met with unemployed in Texas. I visited an AIDS ward with Bishop Swing in San Francisco. I stood with native Americans in Navajoland and Oklahoma City who grieve the loss of their land and their dignity.

A Global Vision: Letter in the Episcopalian, March 1987

In January, I made my first official trip overseas as Presiding Bishop to the Historic Christian Centers of Istanbul, Jerusalem, Rome, Geneva and London. As I traveled and met with the leadership of the Orthodox, Roman Catholic, Protestant and Anglican churches, I was mindful that a significant part of the office of Primate is in helping the churches to listen to one another, to grow in love and unity and to strive together towards the fullness of Christian life and witness.

There are differences not only of theology or ecclesiology. The differences that I speak of are those that find their expression in deep human suffering, alienation, isolation, intense social and spiritual pain that exists because of differences of race, religion, politics, or sex. Differences expressed in a mixture of hopelessness and anger verging on despair—often violence.

Increasingly, through experiences such as these, I see my role as Presiding Bishop not so much as Chief Executive of one branch of the Anglican Communion but as one who must, at least in part, be a channel for the aspirations, hopes, strengths and dreams of our sisters and brothers. For those who seek to live within the vision of the united body of Christ. For those who seek to live free of the chains of political, social and economic oppression. For those who wish to worship in their historic homeland without fear or harassment. For those who yearn to be at one and at peace with both neighbor and all humanity.

The unity for which we pray and the unity that we seek is envisioned in the wholeness and health that is the body of Christ. We may experience many differences but there is one body. We hold to this theological truth. This was affirmed for me on this trip. However, also affirmed for me was the reality that all humanity is one. Here, too, there may be many differences but we are one people—all children of God.

Statement on mission, March 1987

There is strength in our great diversity as a group; the vision is enabled by that very diversity. Our Church is made up of people of many races, cultures, and traditions. Our Church gives evidence of the complexity and perplexity of God's creation. And the life of the Church is inextricably bound up with the mystery which is Christ. For the vision is found, not in the individual parts . . . but in the whole, in the unity and harmony with which the parts, by some great miracle, work together. The Episcopal Church has been called a mosaic of a thousand pieces; but by the grace of God we form one body, one worshiping communion. Episcopalians may better understand the vision by recognizing how our diverse communion works as one and, in turn, functions as part of that Body of which Christ is the head. The vision is not of one part of the Body triumphant, but of all parts united, working together, truly alive.

The danger of excluding ourselves from the wholeness of the body: Address to Episcopalians at the North American Congress on the Holy Spirit and World Evangelism, July 23, 1987

We acknowledge the complexity and the diversity among us. I have listened to Episcopalians for a year and a half now and, believe me, we are diverse! You have got it from the horse's mouth! I believe that part of the role of the Presiding Bishop is seeking to be inclusive. So let us speak and listen and allow the Spirit to move us to a greater understanding of his calling to this church. My real concern, and I lay this on the table, is that we really do not want to include everyone. Sometimes we even make ourselves outcasts and will come in only if we can make others outcasts. I want to say no to that. I want to say that we are all sons and daughters of God. All of us need to be in touch with God for God to make us whole. Offer hospitality to everyone and let God work on each one of us . . .

God works within each of us to make and keep us whole. We must not cut anyone out from a direct relationship with God through his church. The church is God's church and we are called to be faithful stewards of it. We have to preserve its diversity as St. Paul so dramatically reminded us and as duty calls us to remember. Let me repeat what I said in Anaheim. My vision of the church is that there will be no outcasts in this church. Let me add that, as Presiding Bishop, I will do everything that I can to dissuade those who seek to make themselves outcasts.

Address to Executive Council, Pittsburgh, June 13, 1989

How foolish and to be pitied we are to think that our tiny part of the Body is the whole, who imagine the eye can function for the foot or the mouth for the hand. How empowered and strengthened we are who heed the wisdom of First Corinthians, Chapter Twelve, and Ephesians, Chapter Four . . . Without each other, without the gifts of the other, we are weaker and impoverished, less than whole.

Address to Executive Council, Portland, Maine, April 23, 1991

We will come to Convention with many different experiences, many different agendas, many different expectations. It is my hope and my prayer that we will honor those differences, as God does, and that we will, with integrity, accommodate those same differences in a way that strengthens our fellowship and affirms each member of this church. The essence of unity is the acceptance of diversity. We are characterized by our diversity. Will we also be known for our unity?

The interdependence of all parts: Address to General Convention, Phoenix, August 1991

There have been times when the body has seemed out of shape. Usually that has been when, to echo Paul, an eye has said to a hand, "I have no use for you." Or an ear has complained, "Because I am not a foot I do not belong to the body." But that is foolishness, and we are given the grace in our better moments to see and feel the interconnectedness and interdependence of all parts of our body.

Frederick Denison Maurice, the great English theologian of the last century, once said that Anglicanism has a special vocation "to hold together things which were never meant to be separated." I have tried in humility to make this a watchword of my own ministry as your Presiding Bishop. I now know that the landscape looks different from 815 Second Avenue than it did from the beautiful islands of Hawaii. I can see that parts of the body that once seemed quite self-sufficient cannot in fact survive without other parts. "If all were a single member, where would the body be?"

In *The Kingdom of Christ* Maurice noted that the diverse movements in the church of his day were "generally right in the things they affirmed, but wrong in the things they negated." This observation made in nineteenth-century England bears up remarkably well in twentieth-century America. The many movements of our church, the advocacy groups and the caucuses and the synods, are to my mind generally right in what they positively assert and sometimes wrong in what they negate. This is simply to say that while no one group has a monopoly on the truth, advocacy groups spring into existence in order to uphold a partial truth in danger of being neglected or forgotten. We do well to listen carefully to each other, then, even as we resist reducing every mystery of our faith to a simple slogan.

Six years ago I called for a more inclusive and more compassionate church. I declared there would be no outcasts in this church. In the years that have ensued, I have been amazed at the number among us who consider themselves to be outcasts! I have been amazed at the fear that creates outcasts—a fear of difference and diversity, a fear that obscures the faces of our brothers and sisters and makes them seem the faces of strangers.

But the good news is that we have no cause for fear of difference. Difference is of the essence of creation. God created difference, and God called the creation "good." This is a cause for celebration, not a cause for fear. We honor God as we honor God's creation, in all its wonderful difference and diversity.

Today, at midpoint in my ministry as your Presiding Bishop, I renew my call for a more inclusive and compassionate church, where none need feel themselves excluded from full participation for fear of being different. I do this in the name of Jesus, whose perfect love cast out fear, whose ministry was marked above all by merciful compassion and gracious inclusiveness.

Let us dream of a church that refuses to settle its disputes and divisions by legislation, that refuses to accomplish with law what only the gospel can do. What difference would it make if we held in creative tension our partial claims on the truth, trusting the Holy Spirit to lead us into all truth? Would we not thereby hold together [the] things which were never meant to be separated? If it would make a difference, then let us begin by a systematic, critical examination of the way decisions are made in our church. Our life together as a Christian community, our witness together as servants of Jesus Christ and of one another, is too important to be torn apart by binding decisions made in the heat of partisan debate.

Let us dream of a church that recognizes differences as God-given and God-cherished. Let us dream of a church whose members recognize the face of Jesus in those most unlike themselves. Let us dream of a church that resolutely refuses to allow racism a place in its internal life. What a difference it would make! Would not our unity be unshakable?

Varieties of Ministry: Address to Executive Council, New York, November 1991

We have common understandings, fundamental teachings that are central to our faith. We also have different ideas about how these teachings are to be lived out. For example, some want the church to be a place of nurture and support for the faith journey. And it *is* that. Some want the church to be the hands and feet of the cosmic Christ—living out the values Jesus taught and exemplified. And it *is* that. Some want the church to be the vehicle for proclaiming the faith once delivered. And it surely *is*. Some want the church to be a force in the formation of public policy, bringing the Christian perspective to the moral questions before us. And it *is*. Jesus Christ calls his church to be all of these. As individual Christians, we do not all put our emphasis in the same place. And each of us shifts the emphasis during our Christian journey. We must honor the different ways we live out the faith. We must remember that all of these ways are needed and that each proclaims only a part of the Gospel. Jesus Christ needs and uses all of us and wants us to support each other. We, the baptized, are all ministers, and we carry out that ministry every day, where we are. Therefore, a major piece of the ministry of a national church, of a presiding bishop, of an Executive Council is to inspire and empower individual Christians to carry out their ministry in faith, where they are, and in the knowledge that they are not alone.

CONTEXT FOR A PUBLIC WITNESS

The Presiding Bishop received numerous letters over the years admonishing him to stay out of politics. But his own words became an admonition to those who would ignore the role of prophecy in the church.

He began his ministry as Presiding Bishop with a strong appeal to compassion as the foundation for his own witness. Compassion was not only part of his theology, but part of his personal character.

Installation address, Washington Cathedral, January 11, 1986

I greet you on the eve of the Baptism of the risen Christ, so that we too, in the words of St. Paul, might live a new life. Baptism calls the Christian family into a common ministry and mission. I want this to be our day, not just my day, a time for the whole Church, for all the baptized, to again reaffirm its mission for these times. As we begin this new journey together, I invite you to hear afresh the words of God as written in Ezekiel, "I am going to gather you together from all the nations. You shall be my people, and I shall be your God."

As we reflect on the meaning of our common bond in baptism, I am moved this morning to lift up one of the great marks of Christ which we are called to model as the baptized, the mark of compassion that descended upon him from the Spirit in his own baptism.

I want to say to you this morning that I believe with all my heart compassion is at the root of Christian spirituality and mission, and, I would propose, is the hope of our future . . .

Compassion is at the root of Christian spirituality because it was the way that Jesus lived. It was out of compassion, not out of a desire to be in control, that he healed the blind, cleansed the leper, raised the dead and fed the hungry. His spirituality is not one that isolated him, but one that found expression in the service of others.

Compassion is the hope of our future because we live on the edge of the abyss, where our very survival is uncertain. Never before has the human family faced such a dilemma. The fragile earth on which we live is threatened by the very being that God created to be its steward. This is so, and yet there are those in the Church who want us to be only a port in the storm, a haven from the troubles of our time. But God is the Creator, not just of the Church, but of the world . . .

There is pain beyond these cathedral walls which most of us barely comprehend. There are tears of despair which we refuse to see. There are cries for help which we do not hear. There are those reaching out to be embraced whom we have yet to touch. But a compassionate Jesus saw; he heard, and he embraced them. I want to say to you this morning our spiritual lives are bankrupt if our prayers do not call us to see, to hear and to heal. So I say again that compassion is the fruit of our spiritual lives and gives hope to a suffering world.

Compassion is not a matter of sitting apart and from a distance lavishing our blessings on another. It is a matter of entering their world. To know and acknowledge our own brokenness is to understand and share in the brokenness of the world. To understand our own need for Christ who will heal and restore and give wholeness is to know the need of the world in its brokenness and its need for healing, restoration, and wholeness.

Each of us lives out our own faith experiences. For me, it was the discovery of Christ's compassion in my own life that has been the foundation of my own spirituality, which draws me inevitably to my present witness. Remembering our common bond in baptism, I invite you to join me in this spiritual journey of compassion, a journey where I believe faith and mission are inseparable.

Sentimental spirituality of the post-Reformation churches

today can isolate us from our mission in the world. José Miranda has written, "One of the most disastrous errors in the history of Christianity is to have tried—under the influence of Greek definitions—to separate love and justice.

Love and justice. Matthew Fox, in his book entitled *Compassion*, makes this connection for our present-day spirituality. Compassion doesn't make some pastors and others prophets. It makes us both. Being one and not the other should make us uncomfortable. Jesus didn't choose one over the other. Compassion is the bridge between love and justice, between the pastoral and the prophetic ministry.

Our spiritual lives have often been wanting because we have forgotten Jesus' command that we be compassionate as God is compassionate. I want today to call this Church to a compassionate spirituality. When we pray with compassion for those in need, we take those persons into our very beings. They are no longer people who are out there or over there. They now live in our hearts. And once in our hearts, compassion demands that we minister not to them but with them and their concerns.

Compassion calls us to serve the world, not to rule it. I believe that I am called to exercise a servanthood ministry in this office to which I am installed today. Not a servanthood to the powers and principalities of this world, but a servanthood that bows down to the lowest in our midst, to those in the greatest need, to those whom Jesus served, a service to the cause of healing and reconciliation through justice and peacemaking.

It is my fervent prayer today that we claim the compassion of Christ for these troubled times, a compassion that will lead us to a deeper servanthood ministry for the world. What we see in the world today is frightening. Super powers posture over arms agreements while the lives of our children hang in the balance. Unjust governments deny basic human rights while inflicting torture and suffering upon millions of their citizens. We live in an age when we have the technology to feed the world, and, instead, millions are hungry and thousands die every day. Our rivers, lakes, oceans, air and land are being poisoned. Racism runs rampant. It is hard to overstate the horror that we face.

We see a broken world, but our hope lies in a faith that finds God in the midst of that brokenness. Today, we hear Christ speak, "The cup that I drink, you will drink; and with the baptism with which I am baptized you will be baptized" (Mark 10:39, RSV). Our baptismal vows call us to seek Christ in all persons, loving our neighbor as ourselves, striving for justice and respecting the dignity of every human being. That is the motivation for our mission. When we seek Christ in others, we find that humanity is the mosaic showing us the face of God. We move beyond race, beyond economic judgments against the poor, beyond national ideologies, beyond political ideologies.

It is urgent that we be about our mission and remember who we are called to be, the compassionate sons and daughters of a living God, baptized into the mission to which Christ calls us. Our mission may not be what we would always choose, but it arises from the demands of the Gospel in the context of the world as it is. We discover that the God of exodus and exile, of passion and resurrection, is a God speaking through the faithful in the brokenness and fragmentation of Creation.

In speaking of our mission, I offer to you a reflection on my own role. My friends, I have said to this Church that there will be no outcasts. The hopes and convictions of all will be respected and honored. Do not ask me to honor one set of views and disregard the other. I may agree with one, but I will respect both. I say this because, hopefully, we will leave the judgment to God. I may fail some of you as a prophetic voice, but I pray never to fail you as a pastor. I am reminded of this quotation by Dom Helder Camara: "The bishop belongs to all. Let's hope that no one be scandalized if I frequent those who are considered unworthy or sinful. Who is not a sinner? Let no one be alarmed if

I am seen with compromised and dangerous people, on the left or the right. Let no one bind me to a group. My door, my heart, must be open to everyone, absolutely everyone."

The mission to which we are called may be disturbing and threatening to some, but if we seek God's compassionate will in it, it will be for the world our greatest gift. Let us live out a mission that seeks to rescue the world from its present peril, to save those drowning in a raging river of despair, to rescue those caught in a wasteland of hopelessness. Let us commit ourselves to give the waters of baptism to those who thirst for justice. Today, in this Holy Eucharist, let us make visible to a shattered and hungry world a foretaste of the heavenly banquet. In Christ, we have the promise of a New Humanity and a New Creation. In baptism, we are called to become that New Humanity and to build that New Creation.

Mission as Advocacy: Address to Executive Council, February 1987

There is no doubt in my mind that God is calling all of us to a new vision of mission and ministry. And I believe that God's call has a special meaning for Episcopalians. God is indeed renewing the age-old call to mission in our time. The eloquent writer of the Book of Proverbs reminds us that "where there is no vision, the people perish . . . " But the vision of God is here, right now. Our task is to discern its meaning. Certainly it is rooted in Holy Scripture. It is from within this understanding of Scripture that authority flows into the Church. And this authority is found in both the written word and in the action of the living Word as we meet God in our lives. The authority and authenticity of our vision will lie in how faithfully we witness God's great purposes of reconciliation and justice.

The vision shines with the mission of Jesus who was sent by his Father to bring good news to the poor, to proclaim liberty to captives and new sight to the blind, to free the oppressed, to proclaim the year of the Lord's favor. The vision is of the Incarnation, of all of us reaching out with Christ's compassionate hands to our brothers and sisters in need. The vision is one of salvation fused with justice. The mission is in and of Christ.

The vision we are following is not new. And yet each time in history that God has called it forth, it is unique, and compelling in its massive power to transform, to change, to supercharge. This vision can truly change us, transform us, remake us, the people of God, in the image of God.

Address to Executive Council, June 15, 1987

In Jesus Christ, God reaches out to us in word and deed. In our human limitations, we talk of evangelism and social action as separate. In Jesus Christ, they are not two but one. Jesus' words heal and correct injustice. Jesus' deeds proclaim the love of God for all. The message and the deeds of love and justice and victory over whatever resists love and justice are one in Jesus Christ, the servant of God. Throughout the Gospels, Jesus speaks and acts the role of servant. Servanthood is one of the primary images he used to interpret his work. Servant-like evangelism and the servant-like social action are what we find united in Jesus Christ, the Servant Lord. As he tells the disciples when they argue over who is the greatest, "I am among you as one who serves" (Luke 22:2).

Jesus' proclamation of the word of God never overpowers or ignores the unique situation of his hearers. Here is a crucial message for evangelists. Find yourselves in the Servant Lord first. Let his loving presence shape your presence with others. His evangelism is his loving invitation to let him wash your feet and feed you. There are no right or wrong ways in servant-like evangelism. There are only the infinite ways of inviting and encouraging others to eat of the bread Jesus offers and to come among the people who proclaim his loving, compassionate presence in the world. Evangelism begins and ends in prayerful relationship with the Servant of the word of God, Jesus Christ.

Here is, likewise, a crucial call for social activists to be servant-like. Jesus' deeds of healing and inclusion of outcasts and correction of injustice are never contentious. His deeds confront and liberate. They do not pick a fight and they do not put down. They are addressed to specific human needs. The Servant discerns the need and meets it. Our service and work for justice and peace must be his service and justice and peace working through us. Christian social action begins in the love of Jesus Christ and so is most deeply a matter of conversion. One speaker counseled the House of Bishops in 1967: "We must learn to involve ourselves not in our social action but in Christ's social action." . . .

I find signs of growing partnership between evangelism and social action. I find social concern growing among champions of evangelism. I find social activists ever more open to talk of their faith and to draw others to be fed by the same Servant Lord.

Evangelism and social action are not only partners. They demand each other. Each needs the correction of the other. Evangelism and social action must judge and challenge each other . . .

Some questions are put before us. Of evangelists, we properly ask, "Where is your social agenda?" Appeal to the inner life alone is not enough. A converted heart results in a converted life . . . The evangelist must call for justice for the poor and the oppressed and for peace. Not to do so will come across as not really knowing the Servant Lord one proclaims.

There is a second question for the evangelist. Are you doing all you can to help good news be proclaimed in everything the church does? Evangelists cannot withhold themselves for fear of not getting the evangelizing done. Rather, they join the activity and its workers in asking, "How are *we* proclaiming good news? The alternatives are too unattractive and unhealthy when care is not given to proclaiming good news in all we do.

There are some questions for the social activist as well. Are you making your commitment to Jesus Christ clear and offering others the chance to share it as you go about your work? I am impressed by the words of Pope Paul VI. "It is the *right*" of every person "to receive from (a Christian) the proclamation of the good news of salvation." Christians in the public arena do not skulk around hiding their faith and their participation in the life of the church. Yes, we live with others. Yes, we talk their language. We are still able to be ourselves and invite them to the Servant Lord's table. We care enough about non-church people to invite them into the fellowship of love so that they can be fed there too. Even more, we share Jesus Christ because we know the only lasting justice is rooted in the justice of God. Repentance and conversion to the Servant Lord are the real sources of power in the continuing struggle for peace and justice.

The other question for the social activist is: Are you willing to come alongside your fellow Christians whose primary interest is evangelism? Will you stay with them while they deepen their awareness and work out their own agendas? They will be awkward. Stay with them while they learn to walk the way of the cross in deed as well as word.

Evangelism and social action are one and demand each other. We see their unity and interdependence in our Servant Lord. Lord, teach us your union of word and deed.

"I am among you as one who serves."

Address to Episcopalians at the North American Congress on the Holy Spirit and World Evangelism, New Orleans, July 23, 1987

What do you hear when you read the Bible? Do you hear Jesus call you to compassion? Do you hear Jesus call you to include the outcast? Do you hear Jesus call you to justice? When I listen to Jesus, I hear his call to both word and deed. I hear his call in the most profound way possible to proclaim his majesty and to make known his saving grace. I hear his call to include and to care and to be just. To be a follower of Jesus Christ I have to both tell and do.

I grew up in Texas. One of the old sayings that I remember from a Texas farmer is, "You cannot become a Christian by sitting in church any more than you can become a chicken by sitting in the hen house." We find ourselves in Jesus Christ and then we find ourselves in Jesus' ministry of word and deed. That is how we become Christians!

The basic call of Jesus Christ is the call to conversion. You cannot have the Kingdom without the King. Change of commitment leads to changed lives. To become servants of God is to become servants to one another . . .

[Hear Jesus'] call for compassion for the needy and justice for the oppressed. He calls for both inner and outward change. He calls for facing the hard realities of social and political injustice . . .

I have my own stories to tell of learning to recognize Jesus in the works of compassion and justice. I remember standing with the lepers in Okinawa. The two leper colonies on the islands number something like fifteen or sixteen hundred people. Most of these persons, believe it or not, are Episcopalians. In that grace-filled place, I remembered, over and over again, that these persons are the perennial outcasts of history. I remembered over and over again that was where Jesus began his ministry. I believe so must we. I say to you I do not believe that we can close the door on anyone any more.

Let me recall a piece of English Reformation history. I want to share with you something of Thomas Cranmer's life. You know the reformers gave the Bible to the people. For the first time, the people heard Jesus preach something about justice. In Germany, the political leaders did not listen and we had what was known as the Peasants' Revolt. But in England, the church leaders did listen. They called both the rich and the poor to meet at the Lord's Table. They were called at the Lord's Table to resolve their differences. That is, literally, what was happening when Thomas Cranmer compiled the 1549 Book of Common Prayer. Rich and poor were being brought together in confession and absolution. Rich and poor were being fed from one bread and drinking from one cup. Instead of a revolution, the Parliament passed the first Poor Laws of that country—laws that aided the poor, especially in their desire to own and till the land upon which they had been living for centuries.

I want to say to you, dear friends, that our Anglican tradition carries on the same call today. We cannot celebrate the sacrament of the bread of life while people die from hunger. Our heritage of the Eucharist has always pushed us into feeding the hungry and seeking to change the conditions which produce their hunger. I want to suggest to you that our Prayer Book of 1979 is not just another book. It is a tool for mission. William Temple, Archbishop of Canterbury during World War II, summed up our heritage when he said the Eucharist and day to day work for justice are one. Four hundred years later he was restating Thomas Cranmer.

Sermon at General Convention, Detroit, July 3, 1988

What you and I do here, how we live it, and what is reported and heard in the congregations across our Church must be perceived as a clear, clarion call to total mission with the resources and structures necessary to make this mission possible. This mission of evangelism must go out to those who have lost their souls to materialism, who have given their lives to the false gods of success and hedonism, who are wandering in the wilderness of me first-ism, who have fallen into the pits of alcoholism and drugs. This mission of renewal must go out to those who have lost their faith, who have moved to the edges of the household of faith, who have been lured into the stables of authoritarian cults and sects. This mission of outreach must be to the homeless, to those persons living with AIDS, to those under the heel of social, economic or racial oppression. It must touch their spiritual lives, as well as their physical lives. And we must carry this mission to the corridors of power, to those who are the gatekeepers of power and influence. The leaders of our nations must be called into mission, too, to provide the basic necessities of health, shelter, education and food. Our government leaders must be reminded that public policy has a moral dimension and is not purely a secular or political endeavor. The secular and the political can repent and obey the God of justice as surely as the religious.

Suffering with Others: Address to Executive Council, Pittsburgh, June 13, 1989

Two things happen when you travel as the Presiding Bishop. First, you are always accorded the most gracious, attentive, and thoughtful receptions. A steady diet of this and you begin to imagine yourself quite an important fellow!

The second thing that frequently happens is that you are taken to the places of pain, where human beings suffer and despair. I want to bear witness, dear friends: *the pain is real*. The cries of those hurting will not be blocked out by these lovely soundproof hotel walls. The world beyond these privileged gates is too often cruel, hard, and unforgiving. The values of competition and struggle for survival engendered by this world too easily brutalize and dehumanize. In my experience, the Church is strongest and most alive when it chooses to walk squarely amid the pain, its eyes fixed on the wounds of Jesus, whose path took him even unto Golgotha . . .

God is calling us to mission and ministry. God is calling us to be something more than we are: more open, more forgiving, more risking, more loving. God is calling us as a Church to a more conscious role as servant. In many ways the eyes of the

rest of the Anglican Communion are fixed on us—in fascina-
tion, certainly, but also in expectation and hope. In many ways
we are something of a laboratory for the Communion.

A vision of freedom and justice: Address to the House of Bishops, September 18, 1990

Where there is no vision, the people perish . . . Proverbs
29:18a

The vision that built this nation, that made it great, that
reached out to those seeking a new life, was a moral vision—it
was the vision of freedom and justice for all. I want to speak to
you today about this moral vision, and more directly, about moral
leadership.

This vision of peace and justice was not shared with the
native peoples of this country. This vision was never intended
for those persons who were brought to this country against their
will. The narrow focus of this vision has caused the exploitation of the environment, of the laborer, of women and children,
caused international expansion and colonialism, caused isolation and fear of that which is different. We forget these facts to
our peril and frustration, too!

Leaders are great not because of the power of money, or the
size of the military. Leaders are great because of the moral vision they incarnate. Just as we identify the moral vision of
Gandhi, or Martin Luther King, or Nelson Mandela, so, too, we
perceive the moral vision of those leaders who understand, communicate, and act on their moral understanding. They understand
that the earth's rich, varied, and God-given resources are both
finite and must benefit all people. They understand that the invisible economic hand is not the fist of exploitation. They
understand that every global problem has its local victim.

Second, great leadership understands the dynamic and re-
forming power of interaction and interdependence of the various
sectors of society. The effective leader welcomes and encour-

ages the active partnership of the private, public, and nonprofit, voluntary sectors of society. Leadership seeks out the company, counsel, and companionship of the many voices of society.

Third, I believe that moral leaders are under judgment to be faithful to their witness. We ourselves stand under judgment.

The Episcopal Church stands under judgment as a community of faith. The leadership of our church is under divine judgment as servants of the Crucified Lord. We are judged as witnesses of our faith, not of our ideology or our political proclivities. We must always remember who we are—not a political party, not a special interest group, not a political action committee—we are a royal priesthood, we are the church of God.

Our pious platitudes, our fuzzy pronouncements and resolutions, our emotional pronouncements, our righteous sentiments stand under judgment. Our many words stand judged by that one and holy Word, which is "living and active, sharper than any two-edged sword . . . able to judge the thoughts and intentions of the heart" (Heb. 4:12).

Finally, I believe that true moral leadership is prophetic.

Moral leadership gives voice to the quiet whispers of hope. It sings the song of a new land. It cries out of the prisons of darkness. Do I need to remind you, my sister and brother bishops, that the text from Proverbs that stands at the mast of this address is also translated, "Where there is no prophecy, the people cast off restraint . . . "

Where there is no prophecy, the censor thrives. Where there is no prophecy, the racist reigns. Where there is no prophecy, the thieves of liberty plunder the treasure house of freedom. Where there is no prophecy, the charlatans of purity despoil freedom of choice. Where there is no prophecy, anger and hate turn plowshares into swords.

I have learned that all decisions are grounded in moral choices. I have learned of the interdependence of all sectors of society. I have learned about the necessity of being faithful to one's calling. I have learned the power of prophecy. I have learned that moral leadership is grounded in these four marks.

Having put forward these learnings about leadership, let me share with you my moral vision. Let me share with you the dream that helps me to seek wholeness and integration to all that I say and try to do. My vision is both global and local. The many are one . . . It is upon this vision that I fix my leadership.

The basic fact of our time is not independence but interdependence. Hear the testimony of St. Paul: your bodies are members of Christ (I Cor. 6:15); you are the body of Christ, and severally members thereof (I Cor. 12:27); you do not belong to yourselves; for you were bought with a price: glorify God therefore in your body (I Cor. 6:19f); there is one body . . . even as you were called in one hope of your calling (Eph. 4:41); in one Spirit were we all baptized into one body, and were all made to drink of one Spirit (I Cor. 12:13); there is one body, and one Spirit (Eph. 4:4); there is no such thing as Jew and Greek, slave and free, male and female; for you are all one in Christ Jesus (Gal. 3:28).

We are the Body of Christ. This theological vision calls us out of isolation, calls us into community, calls us into relationships. Our vision of being one in Christ makes us whole and forms our spiritual, as well as public, body. Here is grounding of public policy—the actions, the behavior, the programs, the polity we form and advance.

Look around you. We no longer share the moral vision that encourages contribution to the common good. We divide. We uphold the vision of self-interest and self-service. It is paradoxical that as we witness the end of the East-West animosity, at the time of the destruction of the Berlin Wall, we are experiencing a rise of factionalism and racism, of ethnic and tribal tension. We find virtue in denominationalism. We find virtue in individualism. We find virtue in elitism. We find value in nationalism.

In this time of the ascendancy of division, we would do well to stand apart and examine carefully our motives, our policy and action in areas of historic intensity, such as the Persian Gulf. What vision do we serve there? Do we serve the vision of a united world—or do we serve an appetite for oil?

Do we serve the vision of a united world—or do we serve an unbridled Western social, cultural, and political hegemony? Do we serve the vision of a united world, a world of shared resources—or do we serve the self-interest of a bloated lifestyle? Do we serve the vision of a united world, a world made great by diversity—or do we serve a world where the light and darkness clash in personal and international affairs, where Satan challenges the messenger of God?

What is the moral principle that guides our economic system, our trade policy, our national health policy, our national education goals, our environmental policy, our energy policy? What is the moral principle that guides our attention and care of the elderly, the disabled, the refugee, the homeless, the sexually abused, persons living with AIDS? What is the moral principle that confronts racism, imperialism, homophobia, sexism? What is the moral principle, the vision, that animates our public policy? The many are one.

Demonic powers of evil: A message to the youth of the Episcopal Church, July 27, 1993

The scenes come rushing at us through short news clips on the evening news or greet us at the start of a new day with headlines that shock our sensibilities. Blacks attack a white congregation in South Africa. Israel attacks civilian populations in Lebanon in retaliation for rocket attacks and the killing of Israeli soldiers. Sarajevo is under attack and ethnic cleansing continues as another ceasefire is broken. (Just how many have there been?)

Yet in seeing these outrages we are also told that democracy is just around the corner in South Africa. Israel is involved in a peace process with her Arab neighbors. There is an ongoing conference for a negotiated settlement in Bosnia and Herzegovina.

It seems that just when we think something good is about to happen, something awful happens. But that is no coincidence. And the reason is that there are forces, evil forces, which seek to undermine the efforts of today's peacemakers. And they seek to do so in violent and cruel ways.

The motives are not always the same. In South Africa, extremists on both sides, black and white, are trying to undermine the efforts of people of good will. In the Middle East, Jews, Arabs and Palestinians have extremists who see talk of peace as a sell-out. And in Bosnia, hatred is present on all sides, but it is the weak who suffer unspeakable atrocities.

Jesus blessed the peacemakers, but he never said peacemaking would be easy.

We are right to stand with those who must face the forces of extremism from all sides. Despite the cowardly acts of individuals and governments there is much more power with the peacemakers who have joined hands in the struggle for peace with justice: blacks and whites in South Africa, Arabs, Jews and Palestinians in the Middle East, Catholic, Orthodox and Muslim in the former Yugoslavia. It is these people who know that God did not create us to hate and destroy.

Jesus' power was in the sheer force of his love. He had no weapons and he spurned violence. And he changed the world, and us who follow him.

So as we recoil at the horrors we see, at the despicable acts against all that is decent and good, we must be joined with the peacemakers, who, even as the atrocities continue, work tirelessly for justice. They, and we who join them, are the good news behind the horror.

A quality of heart: Address to General Convention, Indianapolis, August 1994

Henri Nouwen talked about community being a quality of heart. And then, in speaking of these next days, he urged us to "take a few risks with your heart." And that is what I am going to do now. I am going to take a few risks with my heart when I say these next things to you.

My friends, I have participated in the Executive Council process that brought us to this place, with the budget proposals that you have before you. It has been a faithful process and a process that has integrity. But I am not happy about where we find ourselves. The proposed program and budget go to the absolute extreme in cutting our mission together. The dioceses don't send them off to "some place else." There is no some place else—and there is no someone else. This is just us.

The money that comes from the parishes to the dioceses and from the dioceses into our national church is for what we want to do together because we are the church together, because we are a community, because we are stronger together, because together we have greater wisdom about how we are called.

We have gone absolutely as far as we can go in cutting back our mission together. Since Phoenix we have cut the legs off of it. Some would say that our financial planning has been prudent. Some would say that it was cautious. I am taking a risk with my heart and saying that we are being fearful. We are not challenging one another.

And while I am taking risks with my heart, I want to share with you another matter that lies heavy on it. Some of the reason for our financial difficulty is because we have allowed our sisters and brothers to believe that it is acceptable to punish the totality of our body by withholding funds from our mission, or by being lukewarm about their participation as a way of saying that they are uncomfortable with the struggling we are doing around difficult issues: sexuality, inclusive language, racism, peace, justice, abortion, capital punishment, gun control, the Prayer Book . . . I could go on.

We have not risen up in the healthiness of our total corporate life and said "No." This is not acceptable. This is not of God. This is not stewardship.

We have cut $3.5 million out of our budget since we left Phoenix. Let us name this for what it is: lost opportunities. The things that would have been done are worthy things. The people who would have been helped, here and around the world, have human faces. We decided in good faith that we did not have the money. But let us say that a little differently: What we said was that we couldn't raise the money.

When we made decisions about our national program, we wanted to share equitably in the hardships felt by dioceses and parishes. This is good and right and proper and appropriate. However, we did not take the next step that I believe is part of responsible and visionary leadership. We did not challenge our dioceses and our parishes to join in the common mission. We did not say, "Here are the needs and the commitments and if we all join in this we can not only do it, we can do it with love and zest and joy." We did not talk about living life abundantly, as Jesus did. We talked about dealing with the pinch.

I say we have cut the legs off of our common mission program. If we cut anymore, if we go below the bottom line of the Executive Council proposal, we will not just have cut off the legs, we will have cut out the heart.

CHURCH/STATE RELATIONS

The issue of separation of church and state was especially important during the Browning years because of the evident partisanship of the religious right. The Presiding Bishop was always clear that the separation issue meant that the

government was not to establish a state religion. Also, the right of faith groups to express their conscience was not to be abridged.

Who speaks for the Christian Community: Speech to Episcopal Charities Conference, May 25, 1995

Perhaps this is a good time to remind ourselves of some basics. Because there are those who think the Church is too political. And I'd like to set the record straight on that.

God entrusted this world to us and made us stewards and in doing so God made us forever responsible for the fate of this earth. That is mission. The Church is only a structure given to us to enable us to do that mission in this world. The Church is a structure that ought to nurture the faithful for the journey of our mission.

Jesus came to save the world, not to save us from the world. And as we experience the waters of baptism into the death and resurrection of Christ, we too become saviors of the world. That is our mission. I believe this is fundamental to who we are and we need to claim it afresh for every generation. And, in fact, we claim it afresh every time we celebrate the sacrament of baptism.

If we are, as the Church, feeding the hungry, housing the homeless, opposing hatred and violence, advocating safe communities for our children, then we are doing mission, not politics. And we need to get clear about that.

I agree with some of my critics that our public witness as stewards often looks political. But that's to be expected. After all, politicians are also stewards of the constituencies they represent. And many of them do so out of a faith perspective.

Where we go astray is if we become partisan. There are those who have said the Episcopal Church is the Republican Party at prayer. Others say that the resolutions of our General Convention look like the platform of the Democratic Party.

We are called to be neither party or any other party. And we must always be vigilant to protect the integrity of the Church against partisanship. At the same time, we must not shrink away from making our public witness because we fear being too political.

And the Church should measure its witness in mission against the common values we hold. If sometimes that means we look more like democrats or republicans on one issue or another, so be it. We have nothing to fear if we are faithful to our values.

Let me say a word about the Christian Coalition. This group is being described as the one of the most powerful lobbying forces in the nation and is given credit for the enormous sea change in the political landscape of our country in the last election. I give them full credit for their commitment, their organizational skills, their fund raising apparatus, and their ability to be heard swiftly and loudly in the halls of Congress. We should take a lesson from them. They are practicing stewardship as they see it. And our own witness is pretty puny when put up against theirs.

One of my quarrels with the Christian Coalition is that they are clearly partisan. They intend to control the Republican Party and have enjoyed a lot of success in that direction. But they risk the integrity of the faith they proclaim because of their partisanship. When their values become the Republican Party's values, they no longer represent a religious voice, but a partisan one. The separation of Church and State by the founders of this country was for the purpose of preventing a state church. That was a wise decision which protects the integrity of both government and religion.

We should not challenge the Christian Coalition in the partisan arena. But we should certainly challenge them. Because some of their values are just simply out of touch with our own. Too much of what they say is based on fear: fear of diversity, fear of women's rights, fear of sexuality. I would hope that our response to the Christian Coalition would be to make a stronger witness of our own values rather than be caught in a reactive or defensive posture. We have so much to say in the national debate and we, along with all the major denominations, need to do it better than we have.

Remarks to Washington Consultation of the National Council of Churches, December 7, 1995

These are difficult times for our public policy witness. Congress is overturning 60 years of social policy designed to care for the most vulnerable in society. The Christian Coalition is perceived by many to be the only Christian voice in Washington. At the same time, many of our churches are struggling financially, cutting back on services, programs, and staff. Despite these obstacles, people are looking for us to be in the debate. We need to find renewed energy and commitment for public policy advocacy, and find more effective ways to do it. The question is how . . .

We need to recapture the language of morality and Christian values. This language has been used very effectively by the Radical Right to justify their policies. But they do not have a monopoly on "family values" or "Christian perspectives." We also speak from that tradition. The problem is that, in our careful attempts to be politically correct and as inclusive as possible, I think we unnecessarily eliminate the principles that make us strong. We are churches. People expect us to use the language of morality, to speak from a faith perspective. We must not be afraid to be who we are . . . "When I was hungry, you fed me. When I was naked, you clothed me. When I was imprisoned, you visited me." These words have meaning in the real world. Let them ring out, loud and clear . . .

We cannot develop an organization like the Christian Coalition. It is an impressive organization, and one to admire for its straightforward structure and political clout. But it is very different from us. We are churches, not political organizations. We are diverse in history, tradition, and structures. We are diverse within our own churches, where both conservative and liberal people worship next to each other in the pews. We also advocate for an incredibly diverse set of issues—welfare, health care, immigration, environment, anti-racism, peace and justice. It's overwhelming. The Christian Coalition doesn't have these diversities. They are a self-selected group of people who agree on a small set of issues. They have one or two spokespersons who are easily identifiable. These are great advantages, politically speaking. It's no wonder we are struggling to keep up! But while our diversity is a limitation, it is also a great asset. We are individual parts that come together around issues of common interest.

Let's focus less effort on structures, and more on our message. Let's reach out to those who are straining to hear us, and those who have forgotten we are here.

The Church and the CIA: Letter to John Deutch, Director, CIA, February 23, 1996

It was with considerable dismay that I read an article by Walter Pincus in today's Washington Post that reports a heretofore unknown fact: "A controversial loophole allows the [CIA] to waive a . . . 19 year old ban on employing clerics or missionaries for clandestine work overseas." This raises a critical concern for church leaders because this not only endangers the lives of church workers but it taints the reputation of all in our field.

Beginning in late January, we have attentively followed coverage given to the report by the task force on "The Future of US Intelligence" sponsored by the Council on Foreign Relations. The panel's recommendation for a review of "the legal and policy restraints" on the CIA, was recognized as having a possible impact on the 1977 ban on the use of journalists, clergy and

Peace Corps volunteers. For churches with missionaries and other personnel overseas, this review is a cause for great apprehension and to read that a loophole has always existed is devastating. This loophole must be closed.

You may not know that the churches played a prominent role in obtaining the ban in 1977 during a period in which an unrestrained CIA was engaged in numerous activities that have subsequently brought embarrassment to itself and to administrations and congressional committees charged with exercising oversight.

In l977, the churches were assured that the new regulations prohibited the CIA from recruiting for clandestine purposes, "any US clergy or missionary, whether or not ordained, who is sent out by a mission or church organization to preach, teach, heal or proselytize." To learn that the restoration of this practice, if it ever was, in fact, not practiced, is under consideration again, goes against all that we believe and all that we can morally condone. The Council on Foreign Relations' recommendation on employment of church workers will jeopardize the lives and security of missionaries and church workers and should not be considered under any circumstance. The recommendation that intelligence agents be allowed to pose as church workers should also be rejected. It is our position that church workers and journalists should be treated in the same manner as Peace Corps volunteers.

Our credibility is at stake and it is every bit as important as the credibility of the Peace Corps. Therefore, I urge that the loophole be closed and the recommendation of the Committee on Foreign Relations be reopened for reconsideration and be rejected.

II
ISSUES

JUSTICE, PEACE AND
THE INTEGRITY OF CREATION

The Presiding Bishop came to see over the course of his ministry that different justice issues had the same root causes. Much of his effort went into pointing to the relationship among economic, environmental and social justice questions (See also the section on racism).

Installation Address, January 11, 1985

I reach out to you to join hands with me in rebuilding the earth, given to us by a loving God, not only to enjoy, but to protect and preserve. In Hawaii, we refer to *aloha aina*, love of the land, and it is a sacred duty of Hawaiians to honor the land. Our mission, too, must be from a sense of sacred duty on behalf of the earth, a world broken and divided and in pain.

Stewardship, the world and the Baptismal Covenant: Speech to Episcopal Advocacy Conference, Washington DC, May 1991

We are reminded in our baptismal covenant that advocacy is a fundamental Christian calling when we accept the vow to strive for justice and peace among all people and respect the dignity of every human being. I am filled with hope when I see this vow moving to center stage of the Church's life today.

I think the vows we make together in baptism are at the core a response to God to be stewards of the earth. I remember in this present age that incredible moment when Neil Armstrong first set foot on the moon. And what I remember most about it was seeing the view of planet earth. It was a moment when we could step back from ourselves and see the world as it truly is—as one integrated whole.

That moment offered a vision of what God intended for all humanity—to be one with all creation. That vision was lifted up by a gifted poet some three thousand years ago who wrote the beautiful Genesis account of the world's origins. His account was as dramatic a view of the earth as the astronauts' view from the moon. "And God saw all that God had made and it was very good."

The poet gives us an additional insight. He says that God makes us stewards of all that God has made. Today I want to affirm the beauty of this world and the hope it offers for us who would be faithful stewards. Stewardship is not a function only for the Church, but a value to be embraced in public life.

I want us all to see this earth as it has been revealed to us, an awesome and magnificent sight which fills us with joy, but also to see it as a fragile place, requiring our care. We as the human race, as stewards of the earth, are not separate from the world, but integral to it. Thomas Berry has said that we will either be in partnership with the earth or we will both perish in the desert.

People are fragile and our stewardship extends to care of the human family as well. When we define stewardship for this moment in history, we cannot afford a dualistic view that pits people against the rest of creation. Our actions must be holistic and all-embracing.

If the vision of the earth seen from the perspective of Neil Armstrong leaves us awestruck with its sense of wholeness, the view from the inner cities of our nation does not. I have seen many other views of this earth during my travels as Presiding Bishop of this Church. I have been in the so called third world and seen immense hardship and suffering.

I have seen evidence of the rural crisis which confronts us and I have seen the poverty and despair present on our Indian reservations. Who of us, in public and private life, does not feel shame at the homelessness we see on our nation's streets? And who does not feel despair that our inner cities have become killing fields.

Our record of stewardship is not a good one. In fact, today, I would offer to say that we have abandoned, for the most part, our responsibility of stewardship. We treat the earth and one another with abuse . . . We continue to remain a nation that controls more than 40 percent of the earth's resources while being less than 6 percent of its population. We define success by how much we consume, measured by our gross national product. This consumerism feeds on itself and demands more consumption which leads to over-production and exploitation of resources. And to maintain this way of life, we justify the expenditure of hundreds of billions of dollars on armaments.

Consumption has come to be a value by which we define ourselves as a people. Remember keeping up with the Joneses? It has been a national motto. What television commercial doesn't offer us status for a consumer society, from the car we drive to the beer we drink to the label of the clothes we wear? I see glossy catalogues that come in the mail filled with useless products, made expensive by a brand name. We have made the financial institutions our modern day temples of worship. The Genesis poet teaches us something different. He says that when God made male and female, they were made in God's image. This is where the Church derives its sense of self-worth for all people. Just to be is to be worthy. If we are made in God's image, we are not only worthy, but holy. However, if our self-worth is based on what we consume, then there is no motivation for stewardship.

And stewardship is more than setting up soup kitchens and overnight shelters . . . The time has passed when our social service agencies can cope with this crisis. We require systemic solutions.

A national foreign policy based on stewardship can give us a new sense of partnership with other nations. A view of one world as seen by Neil Armstrong can teach us that we are one people called to care for the one human family, not a family to be divided by a struggle for wealth.

Consumption in the northern hemisphere has created an impossible burden of debt on the third world by developing countries trying to keep up with interest payments. When I was in Brazil a couple of years ago, an Episcopal bishop of southern Brazil told me: "Yes, we'll pay the debt, or do our best trying; but our children will die, our poor get poorer, crime will rise, drug use increase." . . . Unbridled consumerism in North America mocks the empty stomachs of children in Brazil and everywhere in the developing world where debt exists. Something has gone wrong when developing countries are sending their resources to North America in the form of interest payments at the expense of human suffering. Where is our sense of real stewardship?

The environmental crisis today (fueled by our abuse of the earth's resources), coupled with development needs for billions of people, and billions yet unborn, present an overwhelming dilemma. The problems of global warming, ozone depletion, deforestation and pollution of air, land and water are inseparably linked to unjust economic lifestyles.

We need to move away from defining success in terms of production. Our GNP needs to reflect resources spent as well as goods produced. We need to talk about sufficiency and sustainability. We need to move from seeking gratification for this moment to measuring the effects of our actions on the next generation.

We as a nation have terribly inadequate policies for conservation of energy resources. For years we have lived as if oil was forever. We have been driven by consumption and failed to act as stewards.

Speech to Lilly Foundation conference, October 2, 1992

The value of unbridled consumption both fuels our inner cities' crisis and the global environmental crisis. It is imperative that we see the inseparability of the environmental crisis from the crisis of human need. And the point of inseparability is in the cause. We have been willing to take from the earth without counting the cost to either the earth or the human family. . . .

We are in a fragile balance to provide protection for the earth while meeting the needs of a vastly increasing population of human beings. Environmentalists and activists for social justice must work together to solve the problems we face. I have been deeply concerned that there has been a split between the two issues of economic justice and the environment. They must be one agenda.

A sermon on the environment, April 24, 1994

So God created humankind in his image, male and female he created them. God blessed them and God said to them, "Be fruitful and multiply, and fill the earth and subdue it; and have dominion over the fish of the sea, and over the birds of the air, and over every living thing that moves upon the earth. Genesis 1:27

All of us have noticed that the advertising agencies have gotten on board with the environmental movement. They know that we are worried about the earth, so now when they try to sell us something, they seek to tie it in some way to ecology. They'll talk about how they've changed their packaging to be biodegradable, or how they've started using recycled material in their product. They'll shoot a car ad in front of a backdrop of some scene of incredible natural beauty, and the ad copy will discuss the lifestyle of oneness with nature that you will have if you buy the car. The oil companies, who know that they have a hard sell, take out businesslike ads on the editorial page, in which they earnestly discuss the marine environment and the success of their efforts to eliminate oil spills. A clothing company will include, in small print, a line which tells us that the wooden buttons on its sweaters don't come from trees in the endangered rain forests. An outfit involved in the production of nuclear reactors finds an ecologist for its ad, who poses with her two young children, looking us straight in the eye and telling us that she feels safe living near a reactor. The people who make suntan lotion have never been in better shape; the holes in the ozone layer sell their product for them, and they fill their ads with numbers and chemical formulas and abbreviations which have become household words.

They know we are worried. And we are worried.

In the Eucharist, we tell the story of God's love for us . . . We acknowledge that creation—all of it—was given into our care, and that our self-love plunged us into estrangement from it. We acknowledge that human sin is not confined to cruelty between human beings. Our substitution of ourselves for God has led us to subjugate the creation we love so much to our own sin; just as sin corrupts the relationships between people which God provided for our joy, so it corrupts our relationship with the earth. We are not right with each other. We are not right with the earth. Both those things are part of the same sorrow; we have forgotten who we are. We have forgotten that we are brothers and sisters of the earth . . . We have forgotten that we are children of a loving God. Our God-given dominion has become domination. We have mistaken ourselves for God.

People sometimes criticize the environmental movement for being anti-human, for caring more about owls, say, than about other human beings. They also sometimes criticize it for being racist and classist, seeing environmentalists as people of the elite, who have gotten their overlarge share of prosperity and now wish to deny it to third-world people, to farmers, to workers, all so that they can wear expensive hiking gear on exquisite picnics in an unspoiled wilderness created just for them. We need to face the complexity of this clash squarely and honestly, and assert in a believable way what we know to be the truth: that the love of the earth and the love of other human beings are not two different loves; they are the same. That issues of peace and justice are not fully considered if the claims of the environment are not among them, and that the poor and the oppressed lose much more, much faster in the spoiling of air and ground and water than the middle class ever does. That the injustices done in the history of Anglo and Native American life together, for instance, are not undone by making the Native American a tame icon of an environmental movement that is essentially Euro-American, as if by doing that one were absolved of the responsibility of actually listening to what Native Americans have to say. We need to assert environmental claims as the issues of justice and righteousness for everyone that we all know they really are . . .

Statement on 'Lifeboat Ethics,' February 4, 1988

I have just returned from an extensive pastoral visit to the Episcopal Church in the Philippines. Here I had the opportunity to witness at first hand the tragedy of endemic hunger and human deprivation. Here I was also able to see the work of the Church in ministering to basic human needs, notably through the agency of the Presiding Bishop's Fund for World Relief. My experiences are germane to the topic of what is known as "lifeboat ethics."

Professor Garrett Hardin burst upon the national consciousness in the early 1970's with a paper in *Science* magazine entitled "The Tragedy of the Commons." In it he developed the thesis that, in the commons of a finite global ecosystem (a lifeboat, if you will), those who abuse this should be, to all intents and purposes, exiled from the global community and be forced to reap the consequences of their own folly.

This was essentially aimed at those countries with exploding populations which appeared to be outstripping their food supplies. Mass starvation would bring the population the proper balance with what Hardin called the "carrying capacity" of the land. This led to the concept of triage in which countries that showed that they were able to control population would be helped while those who did not would be left to their own devices. Many have felt that this theory, with its implied callousness to human life, evokes images of the Third Reich.

I believe that there are several reasons for opposing this concept. Theologically, it runs contrary to our concept of the mission to which Jesus Christ calls us. Christians simply cannot stand by idly and watch individuals, let alone whole populations, die of starvation. To do so is to deny the saving presence of Christ in the Eucharist as well as in the very food that we eat. It is to deny our entire Christian heritage of servanthood and compassion. It is to fail to see Christ in the anonymous hordes of the hungry and starving, which is finally, to fail to see Christ.

Second, it implies that there is not enough food to go around. This is simply not the case. According to the Food and Agriculture Organization of the United Nations enough food is produced globally to give every human being on the planet 3,000 calories a day. This is more than ample for the world's population, certainly for the foreseeable future. Moreover, the full potential for growing food in the world has not been attained.

Third, many have identified racist overtones in the thesis. On the whole, it is the white nations who would determine the fate of the non-white. Moreover, there are no real means for forecasting the ability of a nation to feed itself. India, for example, was largely written off in the 1970's as a basket case and today is weathering a severe drought by the fact that the country's agricultural production has increased significantly. It can also be demonstrated historically that the security provided by access to ample food and adequate medical care can help control population better than anything else, with the exception of the education of women.

One might also bear in mind the pragmatic argument that nations would not tamely submit to "hunger blackmail." Robert Heilbroner, the distinguished economist and philosopher, in his book *An Inquiry Into the Human Prospect,* develops a frightening scenario of nuclear blackmail by a nation not receiving enough food assistance.

Finally, the experiences of the Presiding Bishop's Fund for World Relief, as well as other relief agencies, in Ethiopia has shown that the people who survived the famine can, given a chance, become self-sufficient. The Anglican Child Care Program, for example, is helping raise children and teaching them skills to help them become productive members of their communities. The people who suffered from the famine were not passive victims, as they are often portrayed in the media. This raises another question: Should people who suffer as a result of the policies of an incompetent government be summarily condemned to death?

Christian theology rejects Hardin's thesis. It is manifestly un-Christian. It represents a thinly-veiled social Darwinism masquerading as enlightened self-interest. Its only merit appears to lie in a comfortable but specious "out" that it offers to people who want to do nothing.

Beginning at home: Address to Executive Council, Portland, Maine, April 23, 1991

I hope for a serious attempt to simplify our convention lifestyle. I hope we are given the grace to see that an outward sign of simplicity has very much to do with holiness of life and with the mission of the church. If racism is America's most serious flaw, then surely consumerism and a scandalous waste of material goods must rank next.

God's New Order: Remarks to General Convention, Phoenix, August 1991

Now, in a post-cold-war, post-Gulf-war world, the church must not grow timid in advocating for God's new order. Prophets are needed, and God will raise them up, even from among us. These will be prophets who are also evangelists, bold proclaimers of the new life in Christ. Do not shrink from that call when God lays it upon you. It may be a call to resist the spiritually deadly lure of consumerism, which so afflicts our society. It may be a call to resist the corrosive effects of lives devoted solely to maximizing material profit. The communist regimes of Eastern Europe have fallen, but this is no time for triumphalism and complacency in the West. Now is the time for humility, for a great mantle of leadership has been cast upon us as a nation. Now is the time for careful stewardship of the precious life on earth that we ourselves embody. Now is the time to seek and serve Christ in all creation.

Community development: Speech at Lilly Foundation Conference, October 2, 1992

For the Church, the work of community development is simply a matter of carrying out our mission. And that mission is about being stewards of the earth which has been given to us in a sacred trust. Some people might say that the Church's participation in community development is a move away from our spiritual responsibilities to save souls and an invasion into secular matters. There is too much of that kind of thinking in the religious community today. I hope that we can articulate a more compassionate response . . .

The national Episcopal Church has taken about 5 percent

of its investment portfolio (about seven million dollars) to invest in community development projects. I wonder what impact might we make if every endowed congregation, institution and foundation related to the Episcopal Church were to dedicate 5 percent of its portfolio to alternative investments for the rebuilding of our shattered communities? Does anyone here know how much that would be? I know it would be a whole lot more than the $24,000,000 called for by our 1988 General Convention. Many times over. That would be $95,000,000 from the Episcopal Church Pension Fund alone. Add to that what we can do together ecumenically and we will have a real story to tell about stewardship.

Such words from the Presiding Bishop might make some members of my own denomination uncomfortable. But the issue is so right. We desperately need to re-examine our stewardship in response to the world in which we live today.

Statement on NAFTA and its implications, November 1, 1993

Like many of our counterparts in the ecumenical community, the Episcopal Church continues to follow the North American Free Trade Agreement (NAFTA) debate with great interest. As we are witnesses to a time of sweeping change around the world, so we feel the continuing effects of a changing and uncertain world economy. Much seems to be at stake in the NAFTA debate—both in terms of the principle of free trade and in the details of implementing such a potentially far-reaching agreement.

I hear varying, and sometimes competing, voices from within our church on the proposed NAFTA. Many find reason for hope and optimism in the prospect of stronger regional ties and improved economic fortunes for all peoples of the United States, Canada and Mexico. Others express concerns about the effects of relaxed trade regulation upon efforts to protect and improve the environment, protect the rights of indigenous peoples, small farmers, and women, promote worker health and safety, and address wage disparity across borders and the job dislocation and worker migration that result.

Let us continue to be vigilant in monitoring the NAFTA debate and in advocating for implementing legislation which adequately assures that benefits of free trade to countries, industries, corporations, and businesses not come at the expense of the welfare and living standards of real people. I commend to you the principles embodied in the [February 18, 1993] Executive Council resolution as our advocacy work in the church goes forward.

Hard Choices: Statement on the Federal Budget, November 15, 1995

I fervently hope that compassion and civility will extend to our policy choices. The looming debate over the federal budget will show our true colors as a nation. Will we abandon our commitment to those who are poor? Will we restrict health care to some children and to the elderly? A hungry child is no recipe for a balanced budget. Neither is a family plunged into poverty. Neither is an immigrant who is denied essential services. Neither is a mother who cannot find employment.

I recognize that this nation must make some tough choices as it brings its budget into balance. The government simply cannot do all that we wish it could. The Church's tradition of good stewardship with God's resources guides us to make choices that are just and responsible. I am deeply concerned that some of the choices being proposed in Washington are neither just nor responsible. I hope that we, in our daily lives and in our budget debates, will uphold the principle of treating others as we would like to be treated—with compassion, respect, and dignity.

Living Thankfully: World Food Day proclamation, May 8, 1986

In the Eucharist we are called to lift up our hearts to the Lord in thanksgiving. We give thanks for a Lord who stands not against but with; who moves from a posture of compassion not judgement; who gathers in the fragments of humanity that none may be lost.

Thankfulness is the attitude with which we approach the Lord's table in the Eucharist. Regardless of whether we limp or run, we come to that table in the expectation that we will be made one with the compassionate, gathering presence of Christ. The Lord is always there awaiting us with arms outstretched, and He is always there in the form of the steelworker without a mill; the farmer without a farm; the man, the woman or the child without a home; the refugee without a country; all of whom stretch out their arms to us. They, too, are the real presence, and they, too, must be approached with the same reverence, the same sense of thanksgiving, with which we approach Christ's altar.

A young Nigerian priest now living in the United States tells of the first time he tried to conjugate the verb "think." He said, "I think, I thank." Grammatically, he was wrong. Theologically, he was right. Christ said, "Where I am, there shall my servant be also."

COAL MINERS

The Presiding Bishop quietly served as a channel of communication during the US coal miners strike of 1993 against the British owned Peabody Holding Company. This episode served as an example of the power that multinational corporations have in today's global economy and the ability of the Anglican Communion to respond to that power.

Browning wrote to the Archbishop of Canterbury who

brought in English bishops Sheppard and Lunn to speak with the company's corporate executives. Browning also met with the president of the coal miners union and later arranged for him to meet with the Archbishop. Finally, Browning wrote the president of Peabody and made some personal contacts with Peabody board members. The initial response from the company to Browning was dismissive.

What seemed an intractable problem between labor and the company suddenly resolved itself when Peabody moved to the negotiating table and within days reached an agreement, making concessions the company swore it never would. How much influence Browning and the religious community played in this turnabout can only be surmised, but the incident served as a valuable lesson on the potential for the worldwide church to coordinate efforts for justice.

Address to Executive Council, Pittsburgh, June 6, 1989

I went . . . to the little town of St. Paul, Virginia, where the people of that region find themselves embroiled in a bitter (coal miners') strike, with all the anger and deprivation such a conflict engenders. Along with Bishop Heath Light, I went to listen to the stories of the coal miners and their families, young and old, retired and active. We also heard church workers, security guards, and individuals opposed both to the strike and to the church's involvement in the crisis . . . We sought to begin to build bridges and bring reconciliation in what is an increasingly violence-laden situation.

Letter to George Carey, Archbishop of Canterbury, July 7, 1993

I want you to know how grateful I am to David Sheppard and David Lunn, as well as Ruth Badger at Church House, for their wonderful support of our efforts to bring Lord Hansen and his American subsidiary, Peabody Holding Company, to the negotiating table with the coal miners union. The problems we face in the States with coal mines are not unlike those of Britain.

Let me say that I greatly fear the possibility of violence breaking out in our coal mining areas because there are no negotiations currently taking place. It is clear that Hansen is the key player in getting management to the table.

If it fits in with the current efforts of David Sheppard and others, I would again ask you to consider calling Hansen and pressing him to move in good faith to resolve what is becoming an alarming crisis in the States. I make this suggestion to escalate our efforts because of my fear for what lies ahead if negotiations don't start soon.

I appreciate the partnership we have developed on this issue. Our witness for fairness is an exemplary example of our faith in action.

Letter to Irl Englehardt, president of Peabody Holding Company, July 27, 1993

I write urgently to you today to ask that Peabody Holding move rapidly to the negotiating table with the United Mine Workers of America to resolve the serious outstanding issues between the coal companies (BCOA) and the mine workers.

I believe the root of the problem involves serious issues of social injustice which left to fester threaten to erupt into violence in the affected communities. This is a deeply distressing situation. A non-union replacement worker has already been killed trying to cross a picket line.

I appeal to you to lead the way in this matter and to exercise corporate social responsibility in approaching this complicated and disturbing situation. A movement by Peabody Holding to enter into serious negotiations at this time will greatly relieve the present tension that is building every day.

It is certainly not my role to plead for one issue or another in these labor/management disputes, but I will speak for a just resolution of the problems and entreat both sides to negotiate in good faith.

At this crucial moment I also ask that you show restraint and avoid the use of non-union replacement workers. Such an action will only exacerbate the current crisis and I fear for the consequences.

I thank you for your serious consideration of the foregoing thoughts.

GUN CONTROL

In the summer of 1994, just prior to General Convention, the Congress was debating an omnibus crime bill which contained a provision to ban 19 types of assault weapons from the nation's streets. The gun lobby waged an all-out campaign to defeat the bill. The Presiding Bishop, taking time out from General Convention preparations, summoned several of his staff and expressed his outrage that the gun ban might fail. He said he wanted to write an op-ed piece for a major daily newspaper. Within 24 hours the article was ready which, somewhat to the surprise of the staff, was quickly accepted by the Los Angeles Times to run the following day. After its appearance, Browning received many notes from appreciative people, including President Clinton and Sarah Brady, champion of the bill. He also received many angry letters from gun enthusiasts.

The bill finally cleared the House of Representatives but was due for a vote in the Senate where it was doomed to fail unless some Republicans supported it. General Convention was now underway in Indianapolis in mid-August, but the Presiding Bishop, still incensed, called Republican Senator John Danforth of Missouri (an Episcopal priest) to urge him to vote for the bill. Danforth said he hadn't made up his

mind and the Presiding Bishop assured him of his prayers. Later that day, the Senate narrowly passed the bill, with Danforth and three other Republicans, including Episcopalians John Chafee and Nancy Kassebaum, voting for the bill.

Los Angeles Times op-ed on assault weapons and the crime bill, August 16, 1994

I have visited Congressional offices numerous times making various calls on both Senate and House members. Each time I have entered the impressive halls of the members' offices, I have, like everyone, been compelled to submit to a metal detector check to be sure I was not carrying any kind of weaponry that might be used to threaten, maim or even assassinate certain members. This is a sensible practice, given the violence of so much of our society today, and I'm sure is appreciated by the members of Congress.

And that is why I find it so incredulous that so many of these same members in the House of Representatives voted down the omnibus crime bill because they opposed the ban on assault weapons. They surely know what it means to be the potential targets of gun crazed people. Why, then, did they vote against the ban of these terrible weapons knowing that the good people who live in our nations' inner cities do not have such metal detectors to protect themselves from gang violence, violence which is sometimes calculated, sometimes random and always senseless and terrifying?

I ask this question very seriously. On my visits with members of Congress, I have been deeply impressed by the dedication and professionalism of our elected leaders on both sides of the aisle. They are good people, decent, and competent. I think they are often much maligned and misunderstood by frustrated citizens who recoil at the bureaucracy and weight of government. I, myself, have the highest respect for these politicians who deserve better than they get from the general media and public.

Thus, it is all the more so that I cannot believe that any member of Congress could really oppose a ban on assault weapons. Why would we want any private citizen to carry or own such weapons? Of what possible use are they to a civilized society? The fear that these weapons create in our inner cities is well justified by the dreadful actions of those who carry and use them regularly. Surely, these weapons must go! This is a deeply moral issue that is about protecting, rather than destroying, the dignity of human beings.

And yet, people whom I respect and admire and whose company I have enjoyed, voted against the crime bill rule precisely because of this provision.

One member who voted this way told me last year that where he comes from, he has to listen to what people say in his district, and if I want him to support the concerns of the Episcopal Church, he'd better hear from some constituents who agree with me. It wasn't a brush off. In fact, he wanted very much to hear from these people because his true sympathies lie with them. But he also must count votes. And, in this case, the vote count told him to vote against the ban, even though I am certain he would gladly see these weapons go.

But that's not good enough. When a once respectable organization like the National Rifle Association becomes a tool of the weapon makers, and turns into the enemy of reason and threatens the health of our inner cities in order to turn profits, I expect the good people in the House of Representatives and Senate to show them the door and to take their purses with them.

If we need any more evidence for the necessity of campaign finance reform against special interests, we only need to look at the insanity of the vote against the ban on assault weapons.

This is not to say that I am an unparalleled champion of the crime bill. The bill is so complex and embraces so much that no one can like every part of it. If I had to cast my ballot, I would be hard pressed to vote yes because of all the new death penalty provisions. I have never felt it was in the best interests of our society to practice the very thing which we so abhor, the taking of human life. And the evidence has always argued against the death penalty as preventative of violent crime.

If the crime bill fails because some members share my views on the death penalty and vote against it, I respect that. But if it fails because of opposition to the ban on assault weapons, then I weep for the soul of our nation.

President Clinton invited me to have breakfast with him this past August 9 at the White House to engage in a discussion on civility and the role of religion in the public arena. Civility is a word beyond politeness. It is an expression which helps us define who we are as a nation and people. And in a civil society, there is clearly no place for these dreadful weapons that destroy lives and the youth of our land. The President is certainly agreed on this point.

He, too, is a very able man, big of heart and working flat out to improve the quality of life in our country. I applaud the President for refusing to delete the assault weapons ban from the crime bill. Politically, it would be so easy to do. I hope he doesn't back down.

And I hope enough members of Congress can break the strength of the gun lobby and vote for peace and a chance for life in our most troubled communities. Hang in their, Mr. President. I salute you and all those good people in the Congress who know better, and, hopefully, will do better the next time around.

GAMBLING

Gambling greatly increased around the US during the late 1980's, including on Indian reservations. While many in the church opposed the expansion of gambling, some were more open. The national church sponsored a conference in Las

Vegas in 1994 which featured critics and proponents. For many in the Indian community, the issue was about sovereignty. The Presiding Bishop had said very little about the subject because, legislatively, the issue was addressed mostly at the state level and not the Congress. Browning generally was reluctant to speak where local bishops were more properly addressing the issue. But there was one bill in Congress and Browning decided to join other religious leaders on the subject by issuing the following letter.

Letter to leaders of Congress, February 28, 1996

As heads of religious denominations and faith groups, we strongly urge you, as leaders of Congress, to support HR 497, legislation introduced by Rep. Frank Wolf. This bill will establish a national commission to study the impact of gambling. It will also make public policy recommendations.

Legalized gambling continues to spread with astonishing speed and scope—from electronic slot machines to new casinos on riverboats and Indian reservations. We believe a commission is vitally necessary so that a credible and factual study of the effects of gambling can be conducted.

We are concerned, as religious leaders, about the potential impact of gambling on families and communities. Newspapers report that gambling is leading to an escalation in crime and teen-age gambling. In addition, there are reports that compulsive gambling is now a growing problem among adults encouraged by promises of instant riches.

We have seen the effects of gambling in our communities. We implore you, as leaders of our nation, to enact HR 497, so that all Americans can learn about the impact of gambling on the lives of individuals, families and communities.

CHILDREN

The Presiding Bishop expressed his concern over the plight of children at several junctures in his term. He observed with alarm the exploitation of children, first overseas, and then in the inner cities of the US where children killing children became commonplace. To spotlight the problem, Browning invited Marian Wright Edelman of the Children's Defense Fund to address the 1994 General Convention.

During the Stand for Children march in Washington on June 1, 1996, Browning's staff organized Episcopal participation, hosting a breakfast, Eucharist and advocacy training for Episcopalians from around the country.

Address to Episcopalians at the North American Congress on the Holy Spirit and World Evangelism, July 23, 1987

All children baptized at our fonts are our children. But so are all the children out there. We are all one family under God. Let me introduce you to some of our other children in this nation of ours.

There is the young boy so badly beaten by his school teacher that the social worker said if his father had done that he would have been charged with child abuse. There are young people who will have to fight in some future war because only the Army offers them a job and some kind of education. There are children in welfare families that have no greater life expectancy than children in third world countries.

In my home community, many children on welfare are crowded into rooms in welfare hotels—four to seven in a room eating one hot meal a day. They still suck their thumbs and carry stuffed animals at eight or nine years of age. A social worker says of them, "Their needs are not met. They simply don't trust from a very early age. It makes it very tough to have give-and-take relationships later on. They are the future, as all kids are, and it's scary."

The laws and cultural patterns that produce these children are your and my responsibility to change.

Let me introduce you to the plight of children in other nations:

Half the makers of rugs in a district of India are children. Their nimble fingers are faster and cheaper. Children are recruited as bomb throwers in Beirut, Northern Ireland and Afghanistan. Kham Suk, 13, was sold into prostitution in Thailand for $80 because her family desperately needed the money.

We Christians are called to work with our state legislators, our people in Congress and our President to change these conditions. Here in this country, welfare and education are entry points. Overseas, other nations can be asked to enact child labor laws when they seek World Bank loans and access to US markets.

These are global issues. How do they come up on Sunday morning? In Nevada's small congregations, they come up when the people reflect together on the morning lessons. They ask what have these readings to do with our community and our citizenship. In larger congregations, Sunday morning adult classes discuss welfare procedures in their community with a case worker. We Christians need places to try ideas and form opinions. When our country was debating the Constitution in the late 1780's, a Federalist Paper said democracy thrives on the free exchange of opinion. Our discussions in adult class help us chat more responsibly in the supermarket and at coffee breaks. Talking of child exploitation around the world will help us avoid buying products made with child labor. Talking about defense budgets will help us remember that often we make the munitions the children throw. Talking about sexual exploitation of children will help world travelers do something about child prostitution in Thailand.

Such deeds and words delight the Lord. The Old Testament is full of God's delight in us when we do God's works of compassion and justice and inclusion. From Psalm 37, "he establishes (the righteous) in whose ways he delights." Can you hear that delight when the hungry are fed, when children are allowed to be children, and when young people can hope for an education? When we help the helpless, we bring Jesus Christ to them. Christian faith means Christian living. The helpless hear the word in the deed.

Sermon on All Saints', Washington Cathedral, Sunday, November 5, 1995

. . . The child symbolizes the hope and potential of the human race. The child is openhearted and curious. The child's vulnerability has a natural claim on adult protectiveness, no matter what.

But there are people who buy and sell children. There are nations, nations with whom we enjoy profitable trade relationships, in which the worldwide sex industry is a significant factor in their economies. Thousands of children are robbed of their youth for no better purpose than to satisfy the perversity and greed of adults. The vengefulness I feel when I think about this surprises me; I've always tried not to be vengeful. But this ravaged innocence cries out for justice and I am a Christian. I must cry out for justice, too. Whatever has happened to pervert the natural order of things, that causes adults to hurt children instead of protecting them, whatever economic force conspires against impoverished families in developing countries to such a degree that they will sell their children into sexual slavery, whatever psychological brutality has happened in a human soul to make it the soul of an abuser, whatever dimension of corporate greed corrupts a government into disregarding its responsibility for the common good and winking at the sex trade that thrives within its borders like a malignant nest of poisonous snakes, whatever it is that makes these things happen in human society, that is the enemy of all of us . . .

But we need not look beyond our borders for other, more subtle perversities. We are content to live in a wealthy nation in which an unacceptable percentage of children live in poverty. Some among our leaders appear bent on so-called reforms certain to raise that percentage, and they couch their arguments for these disastrous changes in terms of "family values." A hungry, frightened, lonely child is no recipe for a balanced budget. Neither is a family plunged into poverty. Neither is a child whose parents cannot give him the example of hard work and its rewards because they cannot find employment . . .

But God is on the side of all children, the happy ones and the sorrowing ones. May God keep our joy in our children the miracle it is, and may God use that joy to convict us for all those others, those children we do not know but to whom we are also related. Every child deserves that joy, every child deserves that love. The kingdom of God is for those who embrace that joy, whose trust is like that of a child.

Statement on Television Violence: February 29, 1996

I am encouraged by the announcement today that the television industry will voluntarily adopt a rating system to help parents screen violent programs for their children. I, along with many other religious leaders in this country, have long called on the entertainment industry to take responsibility for the kind of programming it shows children. A rating system is a step in the right direction. I fervently hope this step leads the industry not simply to *warn* us about the quality of its programming but to *improve* the quality of its programming.

Violence is a terrible disease in our society. We are bombarded with reports of rape, carjackings, muggings, and verbal arguments turned bloody. Violent crime is rising most dramatically among our youth. It is bad enough that violence pervades the evening news. We must not let it dominate our entertainment, too. The onslaught of violence on television numbs us, and trivializes the moral repugnance of violent acts on human beings.

Violence in entertainment is a deeply moral issue. While it is our *right* as Americans to view what we choose, it is our *responsibility* to teach children that violence is not a morally acceptable form of behavior. Jesus, the Prince of Peace, opponent of violence, calls us to this responsibility.

A television rating system puts us on the path of educating parents and children about violence in entertainment. I pray for the entertainment industry, the government, and communities around the nation in their pursuit of a less violent culture for our children.

CAPITAL PUNISHMENT

The Episcopal Church has opposed capital punishment since 1958. The 1980's saw a rising use of the death penalty in an increasing number of states. In May of 1990 the chairperson of the Episcopal Peace Fellowship called the Presiding Bishop's office and asked him to make a statement about the subject. He readily agreed and issued the following statement several days later. It was widely publicized. The 1991 General Convention adopted it as expressing the sentiments of the church.

Statement, May 1990

Today, I am moved to confirm once again the Episcopal Church's opposition to capital punishment. The church has maintained this position since 1958, and reaffirmed it again in 1979. I take this moment to reaffirm it again for the 1990's.

The taking of human life diminishes us as a people. We all hate the crime of a person who would take another life. But in using the death penalty against the one who has taken a life means we end up committing the very act we found so repugnant in the first place. And thus we are diminished, both in the sight of God and one another.

The taking of a human life, for whatever reason, is an affront to God. The Christian community affirms that all persons are made in the image of God, thus making all people holy. The death penalty is an assault on God's purposes in creation.

The recent wave of support for and use of capital punishment troubles me greatly. For the church, an eye-for-an-eye system of justice has no place. Jesus called instead for a love of neighbor, even of one's enemies.

Jesus told us that the greatest gift we could give is to lay down our own lives for another. Conversely, the taking of another life must be viewed as the greatest sacrilege. The heart of the Christian faith is found in Jesus' offering of his own life, taken by use of the death penalty under Roman law.

In these times when violence is so often used as a solution to violence itself, I wish to align myself with those who are today opposing the use of capital punishment. I commend them for their efforts to light a torch of conscience in our nation. I hope our legislators will want to revisit the death penalty issue and question the increasing use of this sad practice.

Of course, legislators will respond to the will of the people. And I pray God that no politician will again be able to gain election on the promise of support for capital punishment. This is not about partisan politics or vote counting. It is about morality, human dignity, and respect for ourselves as people of justice and mercy.

The church's voice must be heard in this national debate. And, without hesitation, I place my voice at the forefront of the Episcopal Church's opposition to any form of capital punishment.

WOMEN'S ISSUES

Most of the Presiding Bishop's energies in support of women focused on the ordination of women to the episcopacy. This was consistent with his long commitment to women's issues both in church and society. History was made with the ordination of Barbara Harris as first female bishop in the Anglican Communion. Before and after her election, Browning tirelessly advocated full equality in holy orders before such groups as the Anglican primates and the Lambeth Conference. His handling of a potentially schismatic issue may be remembered as one of Browning's crowning achievements.

A mandate from the House of Bishops: Acceptance Speech, General Convention, Anaheim, September 12, 1985

There was an action this morning in the House of Bishops the text of which I would like to share now:

Resolved, That the majority of the members of this House do not intend to withhold consent to the election of a Bishop of this Church on ground of gender and we call upon the Presiding Bishop-elect to communicate this intention to the Primates of the Anglican Communion and seek the advice of the Episcopate of the Anglican Communion through the Primates at the earliest possible date.

Statement on women priests and Anglican-Roman Catholic relations, June 30, 1986

The exchange of letters by Pope John Paul II and the Archbishop of Canterbury, and by the Archbishop and Cardinal Johannes Willebrands, should be read as a mini-dialogue on the question of admitting women to priestly ordination.

The Pope quotes his predecessor Paul VI, who spoke of the

ordination of women as introducing into the dialogue "an element of grave difficulty," even a "threat". The Archbishop says no one anticipates that the path toward full church unity will be without difficulties, and agrees that the difference on the issue is "grave". I believe it would be unfortunate to underestimate the gravity of this issue for the movement of convergence between Anglicans and Roman Catholics.

Serious doctrinal reasons are put forward by the Archbishop and the Cardinal for and against priestly ordination of women. However, a correspondence of such limited length cannot explore the questions deeply, nor reflect all of our current experience. I therefore endorse the Archbishop's proposal of an extended joint study of these issues, using an augmented Anglican-Roman Catholic International Commission (ARCIC).

Episcopalians will wish to express appreciation to the Archbishop for his reporting of the convictions and situation of Anglicans on this issue after consulting the twenty-seven regional primates of the Anglican Communion. On a number of occasions already he has expressed the conviction, which is shared by some other Anglicans, that action should not be taken to ordain women to the priesthood until there is a wider consensus in our churches. A number of Anglican Provinces have already come to a decision on this issue. I would hope that all the churches of the Anglican Communion can continue an open consultation on such an important contemporary question through a process of the various provinces deciding in their synods on the basis of doctrinal reasons, sharing their decisions and thereby helping one another to decide. An example of this process is the recent meeting of the Anglican primates in Toronto where the Archbishop formed a working group to gather provincial responses.

As our churches move forward in consultations and dialogue, I, as Presiding Bishop of the Episcopal Church, uphold two points which are not mutually exclusive. First, we believe in one holy catholic and apostolic church, so we are committed to the ecumenical dialogue for the sake of *koinonia* or the fellowship that should bind it together in the unity of faith. Second the Episcopal Church has proceeded to the ordination of women on the basis of serious and convincing theological reasons which it is willing to share with other churches. We intend not to depart from the traditional catholic doctrine of holy orders, but to expand and open it to the other half of the human race. Like all the authors of these letters I am confident that the Holy Spirit will show us the way forward.

Remarks to House of Bishops, San Antonio, September 22, 1986

There is no question in my mind that the ordination of women, in the experience of the past decade, has deepened for the Church our understanding of the doctrine of grace and salvation. Our church, in a prophetic manner, has made that witness and continues to do so around the issues of women in the episcopacy—it's a witness I earnestly believe will be a contribution of real significance to other parts of Christendom.

Having said this—there is for me another side of that witness, and that is the need for sensitivity for those who cannot accept these decisions. I have met the representatives from this House who find themselves in this position—I have asked that they share with us on Monday. At this point I would just want to say: it's imperative that we find a way to maintain our unity as well as to insure the integrity of our decisions. It's no easy task—it can't be dealt with too early—and, hopefully, what we discuss together will also be a gift to the Anglican Communion.

Statement about the first woman elected bishop, September 27, 1988

On Saturday, September 24, the Diocese of Massachusetts elected the Rev. Barbara C. Harris as bishop. She is the first woman elected as a bishop in the Episcopal Church. This election is an historic event. The Episcopal Church has ordained women to the Sacred Order of Priests since 1977. For many it is the occasion of great joy and celebration. For many it is a troubling time. For all of us it is a time when we will be flooded with deep emotions. It is a time that will test our commitment to the unity of the Church, but more especially our sensitivity to the feelings and convictions of others. It is also a time when we must exhibit a clear commitment to the ongoing mission of Christ's Church, a commitment that must transcend our feelings about this event, however momentous it is.

As your Presiding Bishop, I would like to share with you the canonical process that follows each election to the Office of the Bishop. It is this well tested process that we will faithfully carry out in the days ahead. I want to assure all those unfamiliar with the election and consecration practices in the Episcopal Church that this process is not unique to this particular event.

Experience has shown that the canonical process is not a rubber stamp. The process is not an institutional shortcut or a deterrent to prayerful, thoughtful discussion. Every Episcopal election is the occasion for the Church—through the electing dioceses, the Standing Committee of every diocese, and the bishops with jurisdiction—to renew its biblical, theological, and ecclesiological understanding of the apostolic ministry. This canonical process offers the Church an ongoing occasion for continuity, renewal and, if it be God's will, a reformation of its clerical leadership.

During the next days there will be many participants in the consent process. Some will be exercising their canonical responsibilities and others will be providing the context for the local decision-making through the sharing of information and opinion. My role in the process as Presiding Bishop is clearly defined by the canons and I am committed to the faithful execution of this role.

There is a role for every Episcopalian and for those who join us in worshiping and serving God. Our offering will be in our prayers. This is a time for us to offer our joy, our anxiety, our commitment to unity to God in prayer. For discernment, for guidance, for patience and understanding, for God's grace that makes community possible and hopeful, this is a time for prayer. It is the witness and admonition to prayer that we have in the testimony and action of the Apostles. It is to prayer that I call the Episcopal Church in response to this historic action.

Ecumenical implications: Statement, February 8, 1989

As I noted in my letter to you of September 27th, the Rev. Barbara C. Harris has been elected Bishop-Suffragan of the Diocese of Massachusetts. The required canonical process following her election has now been fulfilled, in that the election has been consented to by the majority of Diocesan Standing Committees and Bishops having jurisdiction. I will ordain her to the episcopate on February 11th in Boston. I ask your prayers for the Bishop-elect, for the Diocese of Massachusetts and its Bishop, and for The Episcopal Church and Anglican Communion.

For twelve years, our Church has experienced the gifts of women in the priesthood. It is our hope, prayer, and clear expectation that we will have a similar experience with women in the episcopate. We believe that the incorporation of women in the catholic episcopate and priesthood as the Anglican Communion has received it, enhances the wholeness and the mission of the Church. I pray that their inclusion will come to be seen as a gift to the Church catholic and a contribution toward a deeper understanding of holy orders.

The Episcopal Church seeks to maintain and develop the highest possible degree of communion with partner churches. We have taken every reasonable step. Within our own Church we have sought pastoral provisions for those who cannot accept women in the episcopate. Within the Anglican Communion the Archbishop of Canterbury has appointed a commission to prepare guidelines to enable Provinces which differ on this issue to live together in one Communion. Ecumenically we have consulted with the several partner churches through official dialogue.

We rejoice in the growth of communion in recent years with Orthodox, Roman Catholic, Lutheran, and Protestant Churches. Yet the road to Christian unity is not a straight line. The question of women's ordination, in the form in which it is put today, is a new one, and is still in an early stage of reflection and discussion among the churches. Given the complexity of the process which must take place, discussion will be the experience of a more active participation by women in the life and mission of the Christian community.

Our ecumenical dialogues will be driven to a deeper theological seriousness as a result of the ordination of women to the episcopate. In dialogues with Churches that maintain the historic episcopate we should concentrate on the serious theological reasons for opening the historic episcopate to women. In dialogues with Churches that do not claim to have the historic episcopate we should show how teaching about the catholic episcopate is compatible with the ordination of women.

At this moment, our action brings rejoicing to some and anguish to others. The Lambeth Conference spoke directly to this situation when it resolved, "The Church needs to exercise sensitivity, patience and pastoral care towards all concerned." We remember, too, that within the one holy catholic and apostolic Church some suffer pain because women are excluded from the episcopate and priesthood, and others suffer pain because they see ordination of women as a violation of God's will. I ask that we enter into one another's pain so that the fellowship of suffering may become, together with the fellowship of rejoicing, a sign of our deeper communion and a witness to the healing of the nations.

Anglican implications: Address to Executive Council, Pittsburgh, June 13, 1989

Just before leaving for Central America I met with the Eames Commission on Long Island. This was the crucial first meeting of the Archbishop of Canterbury's Commission on Communion and Women in the Episcopate after the consecration of Barbara Harris as bishop. Also meeting the commission on Long Island were Bishop Harris and other ordained women from Canada and the United States, as well as representatives of the Evangelical and Catholic Mission. The sensitive listening and hard work of the commission bore much fruit when its recommendations were presented to the Primates in Larnaca.

Let me just say that in spite of the pace and crowded agenda of the Primates' meeting, I found it a time of great encouragement and refreshment. Especially encouraging was the report of the Eames Commission, which most if not all of you will have read by now and which was enthusiastically accepted by the Primates, with the one significant exception of the suggestion for so-called "collegial ordination." Many found the show of unanimity on the part of the Primates surprising; it was certainly heart-lifting. Encouraging too was the optimism of the report about our Communion's ability to maintain the highest degree of unity in the face of differences in principle and practice on the ordination of women to the episcopate. As I said in my recent pastoral letter, I believe the Eames Report has significance not only for improved relations with the Anglican Communion, but good news for our Church as well. The House of Bishops will now consider the Eames Report in the light of our own unique situation.

I have heard the pain of ordained women in our Church, whose ministries are yet the subject of debate and equivocation. This is not right! The gifts of ordained women in ministry are too precious, too tempered and true, to be questioned and derided. Their pain is our pain until God's gift of ministry in baptism is recognized as natural and efficacious, blowing where the Spirit wills it, calling forth prophets, priests, and pastors from the rich treasure house of God's people.

But I know the pain, too, of many in Fort Worth a few days ago. Unhappy and bewildered over the changes of the past decade, they have reached the point of crying, Stop! Listen to us! You have ignored us, cut out from under us our faith, taken our Church from us! Their pain, alienation, and anger at times have seemed irredeemable.

In our own beloved Anglican Communion, the search for *koinonia* is made more difficult by that great divide in consciousness that is the hallmark of our time. I would describe the divide as that between those who tend to see tradition as a dynamic reality and who therefore accept the possibility of continuing revelation, as over against those who tend to see a once-for-all-ness in the divine dispensation. The divide is not a neat one, and we are all probably a bit schizophrenic in finding ourselves first on one side and then the other as we face different questions and dilemmas. The divide in consciousness threatens our Communion most severely today over issues of authority, sexuality, and the ordination of women. And yet I maintain—as have the Primates—that we need each other for the integrity and the *whole* Church's unity, witness, and mission. For it is a sad but very human fact that those on one side of the divide run the risk of being too much caught up in the deceptive and shifting winds of the times; while their brothers and sisters on the opposing side run an equal danger of being so caught up in attending to internal ecclesiastical order that they miss God's hand in the movement of history. If we accept as an article of faith "One Lord, One Faith, One Baptism," then common sense tells us we need each other for mutual correction and that we therefore should, in the words of the author of Ephesians, "spare no effort to make fast with bonds of peace the unity which the Spirit gives."

Respecting the opinions of those who differ: Remarks to Executive Council, Pittsburgh, June, 16, 1989

In my address from the chair on Monday, I said that I would have some things to say about the gathering in Fort Worth earlier this month called by the Evangelical and Catholic Mission . . .

I declare my unshakable belief that God is calling us to maintain our unity, even in the midst of our diversity, our tension, and our pain. I believe with all my heart that the unity we have in baptism is a gift whose preciousness we dare not squander, for it is a unity bought with the very blood of Christ.

With regard to the meeting in Fort Worth, I cannot overemphasize my belief that those who disagree with the majority must not be marginalized in our Church and will not be. This is not a political strategy. This is a theological necessity.

We have worked to keep an open climate in our Church. This climate of openness is healthy and necessary. It was this climate that allowed the 1,200 or so individuals who gathered in Fort Worth to air convictions about the ordination of women, even though they are contrary to the prevailing understanding of the people of the Episcopal Church and the decision of the General Convention. I take seriously the issues raised at Fort Worth, and I take seriously the people who raised them.

We are part of the worldwide Anglican Communion, as well as the larger Christian community. For this reason, we have always sought not to act in an arbitrary or isolated way. Indeed, the process that has brought our Church to make canonical provision for the ordination of women to the priesthood and episcopate has been recognized and affirmed every step of the way by successive actions of the Lambeth Conferences of Anglican bishops, by meetings of the Anglican Consultative Council, and by the Primates of the Anglican Communion. Because of this careful process, I believe we have much to offer other provinces (of the Church) now moving toward decisions on women's ordination we made in 1976.

Most recently, the Anglican Communion has spoken through the Archbishop of Canterbury's Commission on Communion and Women in the Episcopate (the Eames Commission). The report of the commission was affirmed by the Primates last month at their meeting in Cyprus. I remain convinced that the reflections and guidelines contained within that report provide the context for living with differences of opinion while maintaining the unity and mission of the Church. The commission's work will continue, and we will continue as a Church to be informed by their insights and guidance.

In three months, the House of Bishops will meet in Philadelphia. Central to our discussions at that meeting will be the consideration of the Eames Commission report and the Primates' statement . . . However, the issues before us concern the whole Church, not just the Presiding Bishop or Executive Council, not just the House of Bishops or General Convention. I therefore call on all Episcopalians to pray and work for the unity of our Church, respecting the opinions of those who differ and finding room for all who seek to be faithful followers of Jesus within our beloved tradition.

Address to Executive Council, Minneapolis, June 15, 1993

. . . There are persons of good faith in our church who remain unconvinced of the theological rightness of the ordination of women. These hands that consecrated Barbara Harris and Jane Dixon were also placed on the head of Jack Iker. And God was there in all of that.

The Ecumenical Decade of Churches in Solidarity with Women: Article in *Episcopal Life*, May 1992

We are all God's children. We are brothers and sisters in

Christ. Therefore, in a profound sense, all of the world's mothers are our mothers. All of the world's children are ours. Our Christian journey is leading us from the particular of our personal family into the whole human family.

This painful truth of the world's mothers and children was spoken of again and again at the Worldwide Anglican Encounter in Brazil this spring. This Celebration of Life for a Reign of Justice and Peace was part of the Ecumenical Decade of Churches in Solidarity with Women. Searing stories were told of violence against women and children, violence done to their bodies, to their minds, to their hearts and souls. We heard from women isolated and disempowered by structures that affirmed and supported only males. We also heard from women who have survived, whose spirits—yoked with the spirit of Christ—have become strong in adversity, but too often they have paid a terrible price for their survival.

In view of these grim realities, it is alarming that the Ecumenical Decade of Churches in Solidarity with Women, sponsored by the World Council of Churches, is receiving so little attention. The decade, which began in 1988, has brought some welcome changes. At the same time, many Christian men have a hard time seeing women's issues as their issues. And many of us, women and men, have a hard time seeing, believing, and acting as if we had a responsibility for all the mothers of the world and their children.

It is not too late. There are signs of hope. Churches have learned that we can be particularly effective working to increase awareness of the plight and needs of mothers and children. Around the church, faithful people are working regionally and nationally for education and legislation, challenging and cooperating with lawmakers, boards of education and health, making our Christian witness.

Bishop Steven Charleston of Alaska offered hope to the encounter when he said that the light of the church is beginning to grow in the darkness. That light, he said, was reflected in every woman at the encounter. I saw that light. I see it all around in the church, growing stronger. I believe that if we each bring our own candle to the darkness by acknowledging our loving responsibility for the mothers and the children, then our light can banish the darkness.

ABORTION

The issue of abortion arose several times during the Browning years. Members of The National Organization of Episcopalians for Life (NOEL) regularly called on the Presiding Bishop to condemn the practice. After the General Convention of 1988, he routinely supported the resolution approved at that convention and a slightly amplified version adopted in 1994.

In 1994 he signed with others a letter which called for the protection of the rights of women to reproductive services, including abortion, in any health care bills before the Congress. He received a great many angry letters from pro-life advocates.

In 1996 President Clinton vetoed the so-called partial birth amendment and was vilified for it by, among others, the US Roman Catholic cardinals. Bishop Browning joined a group of other religious leaders supporting the president's action. Later, Browning wrote a follow-up letter to the President to clarify the Episcopal Church's position on abortion.

Address to Episcopalians at the North American Congress on the Holy Spirit and World Evangelism, July, 23, 1987

I would like to focus—as a way into the plight of children—on the plight of the unborn child and on the issue of abortion.

Still again, let us begin with the biblical and the theological. Too often we sound like the world around us. Robert Bellah, an Episcopal sociologist, has reminded us how much Americans are consumed by individualism—a desire to be ourselves and to advance ourselves with little regard to others except as aides on our way to self-actualization. Much of our talk about abortion seems to be flavored by these themes of self-expression and self-advancement. In the world, and often within the church, we talk about pregnancy as a private matter. We take a fresh start biblically when we say that pregnancy is a community matter. The birth of Jesus was a tremendous community event. There were shepherds and wise men and animals and angels—the whole created order was in on it! In Baptism, we say these children belong to the whole congregation. An unmarried pregnant woman is a community concern. Call the community to support her and let the community call the father to care for the child. If we treat her as an individual problem, then we will find an individual solution. For Christians, pregnancy has to be a community problem calling for a community answer.

There is a small congregation in Southern California and there is a large congregation in Northern Virginia seeking to live this way. There are many more. These people have opened their homes to young women outside their congregations who have been told to leave home if they will not have an abortion. They have families taking in unwed mothers for the last months of pregnancy and the first month with the new baby who is then given up for adoption. A 14-year-old in one of the families said, "I resented my family, making me share with another, but I loved that baby like my own sister when she left." These are signs of what community response might be. They are powerful signs. I could get interested in belonging to a church like that! There are great words of good news in these deeds.

Let me say that there are painful stories too. Who has not known the pain of walking with those who have chosen abortion because the health of the mother or the child was threatened?

There is the more painful story of aching over people seeking abortion for convenience. Even more, there is the terrible, painful story of abortion brought on by tremendous poverty and the stress that poverty causes to so many people within our communities.

Now the Episcopal Church in past conventions has said a number of things. It has tried to affirm the woman as having the responsibility and accountability in that decision. We have also said that decision should never be taken without consultation with representatives from the community. I want to say to you that the opportunity exists, therefore, for the community to provide pregnant women with reasons and resources for the continuing life of the unborn rather than the termination of that life. I am asking you to help me to manifest that in the congregations to which we belong. Unless we are willing to do that, it is just so much rhetoric.

You know it is very difficult to be non-judgmental with one another. I have wondered at times of those who have walked with Jesus. His companions included lepers, prostitutes and tax gougers. I wonder if we let ourselves be found in his and their company.

I believe abortion is a community concern. But I also believe that does not deny or deprive the right, the responsibility or the accountability of the woman. In all, I hear Jesus Christ's call for inclusiveness and compassion and justice.

Responding to Supreme Court rulings on laws limiting abortion rights, July 11, 1989

The recent ruling of the Supreme Court of the United States on abortion has brought this subject to the forefront of our national conscience. News reports of action and reaction are much before us. People are taking sides, drawing lines. In such a climate complicated moral questions are inappropriately reduced to simple rights and wrongs, pros and cons. Such simplistic reasoning is not true to our understanding of our faith.

As Christian people we stand in awe and reverence at the mystery of our life as God grants it. We know that, at its heart, abortion involves a tragedy, as the loss of any life or promise of life can be tragic. The reasons for abortion can involve other tragedies. Our discussion of abortion must begin with an understanding that we are dealing with a tangled web of rights and wrongs, good and evil, and greater and lesser tragedies. Our discussion of abortion must take place within a larger framework which includes issues of human sexuality and family life. Our discussion of abortion must focus on finding what can be redemptive in an already broken situation.

It is in these understandings that the position on abortion of the 1988 General Convention of the Episcopal Church was forged. I use the word "forged" quite intentionally because the people of the Episcopal Church represent a spectrum of opinion on this issue. Our legislation was passed after a creative time of study by the Commission on Human Affairs and Health and respectful listening to one another.

The legislation adopted by the General Convention stressed the sacredness of human life, the legal right of a woman to a medically safe abortion, opposition to abortion as a means of birth control, family planning, sex selection or convenience. The General Convention also expressed its conviction that any action by national or state governments must respect individual conscience and decision making. It condemned all actions of violence against abortion clinics or against those seeking services at such clinics.

It is my hope and prayer at this time that members of the Episcopal Church will enter into these discussions and bring to them the insights of our faith. It is my hope and prayer that all people of faith will engage in the debate in a spirit of openness and respect for the views of one another.

Letter sent to persons inquiring about support for reproductive health services in health care reform, 1994

. . . It is inaccurate to characterize my opposition to denying customarily provided health insurance benefits in any area as contradicting the 1988 General Convention resolution on abortion. The Spring, 1994, issue of *NOEL News,* in the article "NOEL prepares for General Convention," itself notes that " . . . There remains much more to be done: the Church still acknowledges 'the legal right' of every woman to an abortion . . ."

This makes the point precisely. To the extent that the 1988 resolution speaks to the public policy arena, it "acknowledges that in this country it is the legal right of every woman to seek a medically safe abortion." It also affirms that "individual conscience is respected, and that the responsibility of individuals to reach informed decisions in this matter is acknowledged and honored." Insurance companies currently provide for reproductive health services so that, should a woman's individual conscience lead her to avail herself of those services, she will have access to medically safe services. Health reform legislation seeks to extend health insurance coverage to all, not restrict currently customary coverage in a particular area.

Of course, the 1988 resolution primarily addresses persons within our Church—persons who freely and voluntarily choose to be Episcopalians. Yet, when it does speak outwardly to the larger arena of public policy, as your own publication points out, it expects women choosing abortion to continue to have access to medically safe abortion.

Letter to President Clinton from Browning and other religious leaders, April 29, 1996

As mainstream religious leaders, we write to express our agreement with your veto of HR 1833, the so-called "Partial Birth Abortion Ban," and we are urging Congress not to override that veto. We know that some religious leaders have criticized you for that veto based on their sincere religious beliefs that human life is sacred. You should know that we, too, hold human life sacred, yet we respectfully disagree with this legislation. We fully support your action in standing with women and their families who face tragic, untenable pregnancies.

In the case of several fetal anomalies of threats to the life and the health of the mother, people of faith are called to cherish the life of the mother and others who are affected—the husband or partner, the children already living, and others—and to have compassion for a fetus who, if born, would inevitably suffer to die.

We are convinced that each woman who is faced with such difficult moral decisions must be free to decide how to respond, in consultation with her doctor, her family, and her God. Neither we as religious leaders, nor you the President, nor Congress—none of us can discern God's will as well as the woman herself, and that is where we believe the decision must remain.

Indeed, where religious people have such profound and sincere differences—even within our own denominations and faith groups—the government must not legislate, and thus impose, one religious view on all our citizens. To do so violates our most cherished tradition of religious freedom.

Thank you for your leadership, courage and compassion.

Letter to President Clinton, May 8, 1996

As you know, I joined other mainstream religious leaders in supporting your veto of the "partial birth abortion" ban. I continue to support your decision on this extremely difficult issue. While there continues to be a great deal of misinformation and confusion about this particular medical procedure, I would like to clarify the Episcopal Church's teaching concerning abortion.

Amid great disagreement and prayerful deliberation on the issue of abortion, the Church's 1994 General Convention, the highest legislative body, adopted a position that states "all human life is sacred from its inception until death" and stresses that "we regard abortion as having a tragic dimension, calling for concern and compassion of all the Christian community." . . .

The Church's position recognizes that legislation concerning abortion will not address the root of the problem; rather, a decision by a woman in this Church should be instructed by her own conscience in prayer and by seeking advice and counsel of members of the Christian community. The Church expresses "its unequivocal opposition to any legislative, executive, or judicial action . . . that abridges the right of a woman to reach an informed decision about the termination of pregnancy or that would limit the access of a woman to safe means of acting on her decision." I have enclosed the full text of the Church's position.

Mr. President, I know that this is a tremendously difficult issue for you as it is for the country. I thank you for this opportunity to share the position of the Episcopal Church.

HUMAN SEXUALITY

No issue has been more divisive in the church than that of homosexuality and the reader will note in the many writings of Bishop Browning his unfailing efforts to hold the church together during this tempestuous time. Many times he set aside his personal views and declined to be an advocate for one side or the other, choosing instead to hear the pain of both sides and offering himself as a pastoral channel for the church to discuss the issue. While some bishops and others accused him of thinly veiled support for gay ordinations, members of the House of Bishops praised him at their 1995 meeting for his pastoral sensitivity in reaching out to all sides.

Consistent with his view that there shall be no outcasts, he attended and preached at an annual meeting of Integrity (an Episcopal advocacy group for gays and lesbians and their friends) in July, 1992, and in 1996 preached at a meeting on gay and lesbian ministry in New Jersey. The latter occurred shortly after an ecclesiastical court had ruled that there was insufficient doctrine to try a case against the Rt. Rev. Walter Righter for ordaining an openly gay priest.

Toward the end of his tenure, Browning began to advocate more openly for gays and lesbians. In an address to Executive Council in June, 1996, he declared his belief that gays and lesbians in a committed relationship could be wholesome examples. Several dozen conservative church members took out an ad in the Washington Times to protest his statement.

When he attended the World Council of Churches Central Committee meeting in September, 1996, he insisted that the WCC engage in dialogue about the issue against the expressed wishes of the Orthodox churches.

Browning also tried to help the church differentiate between sexual misconduct—which could be both heterosexual or homosexual—and sexual orientation.

However torn the church may be internally over sexuality, especially homosexuality, the church has maintained support for the civil rights of gays and lesbians since 1976. In this arena, Browning never hesitated to support efforts to affirm those rights, including joining his name in support of a civil rights bill for gays and lesbians in the US Congress. He attended a press conference for the bill on September 5, 1996, at the invitation of Senator Ted Kennedy. Much to everyone's surprise, the bill failed by only one vote in the Senate, 50-49.

At the time of the Pentagon's decision to revise its policy on gays in the military, his sense of fairness led him to issue a strong condemnation of continuing an unfair bias.

He also filed an *amicus* brief at the Supreme Court in

1994 to oppose Colorado's constitutional amendment allowing discrimination against gays and lesbians. The amendment was struck down by the court.

Letter to *The Witness*, July 1986

. . . It is my experience that little is really understood about homosexuality. There is diverse professional opinion about its genesis, and there are historic myths about the homosexual condition. The persistent lack of real communication on this human condition has fostered mutual distrust between heterosexuals and homosexuals. This distrust has caused separate communities and created walls of misunderstanding. No ghetto is spiritually healthy, and that includes the sexual ghetto.

We cannot ignore nor treat lightly the fact that the Church has understood and taught that marriage is the norm of sexual expression. Roger Shinn, the noted Protestant theologian, has stated it succinctly, "the Christian tradition over the centuries has affirmed the heterosexual, monogamous, faithful marital union as normative for the divinely given meaning of the intimate sexual relationships." In the New Testament selected passages seem to pass judgment on homosexual actions and relationships. I am well aware of those who are ready and armed with these proof texts when discussing this subject. There are many within our Anglican tradition, as well as the other Christian traditions, who can speak with authority on the biblical and theological aspects of homosexuality. There are many exegetical approaches and conclusions about the total witness of Holy Scripture on this subject. I hear you asking me for a pastoral response.

First, I believe that no one should stand between a person and our Lord Jesus. I have tried to establish a pastoral ministry which brings people to Jesus. It is in relationship to Jesus that we find our true selves and know God's will for us. The Christian must be careful not to call into question another's faith by prejudicial harshness. It is our apostolic ministry of compassion which fosters relationship with God through the forgiveness of Jesus.

Second, I believe that the Church must foster reconciliation. Through word and sacrament, the Church can be a loving and reconciling force in the world. Every human being needs love and reconciliation. We must never assume that any one of us is without sin or above the need for penance and reconciliation.

Third, I believe that Jesus' sacrifice for our sins put our guilt and self-rejection within the healing presence of hope and grace. My vision of our Church is that of a community where love and grace abound.

The Church is well aware of my participation in the statement of conscience in response to the resolution concerning the ordination of homosexuals which was passed at the 1979 General Convention. Few, however, have heard all my reasons for opposing the legislation adopted. I have been consistently on record in the House of Bishops opposing those attempts to constrict the established canonical processes granted to the dioceses. In the matter before the General Convention in 1979, I believed that the freedom of the Diocesan Commissions on Ministry was being circumscribed. The duties of the Diocesan Commission and the Bishop are clearly outlined in Title III of the Canons. I believe that these canons give ample guidance to an ordination process that encourages all parties to seek God's call and will, and that should not be encumbered. I continue to hold to that position.

I look forward to growing more conversant with this issue and I encourage the Episcopal Church to gain a greater perspective on homosexuality and to explode and transcend the myths and phobias which impede our common life.

I welcome this opportunity to share these thoughts with you. I hope that they will contribute to a reasoned reflection and discussion within our Church. I do not believe the issue will be resolved quickly, but I pray that the process ahead will be conducted with the awareness that it is done in the presence of our blessed Lord.

Letter to *The Witness*, January 1987

I have read, reread, and pondered long and hard upon the responses to our exchange of letters which appeared in the September issue of *The Witness*. I would like to share a few thoughts which have emerged.

I want to thank *The Witness* for providing a forum for the public discussion of homosexuality. I am gratified by the response to our published correspondence. Many sent me personal letters. I have read all, and I hope that they are but a small indication of the dialogue within the church. I am pleased that the concerns expressed in each letter have been lifted up. I am intensely moved by the anguish conveyed. And I am encouraged by the remarkable vulnerability several writers were willing to risk. . . .

I must candidly remind you that our church is of many minds about the place of homosexual people in Christendom. Since my remarks at the Los Angeles Convention, I would suspect that I have heard every possible position. Some Episcopalians on *both* sides of this issue hold views that reveal prejudice, myth, misinformation and spiritual shallowness. On the other hand, some communicants' views—again on both sides—are based on careful thought, extensive study and serious soul-searching. The painful truth is that we are not, as a church, reconciled about whether gay and lesbian people, while "children of God, fully deserving of the pastoral care and concern of the church" (from 1976 General Convention resolution), should be admitted to Holy Orders or whether their sexual unions should be blessed by the church. . . .

As Chief Pastor I want to say that I am grieved by this brokenness in our church. I am in no way insulated from the anguish of gay and lesbian Episcopalians in a church that is torn over how to treat them. Many have shared with me their heartrending stories; I have ached with gay clergy and lay people who have been treated with hostility by parishes and dioceses. They have paid an enormous price at times as they tried, in good conscience, to lead integrated Christian lives. I am appalled by the violence against homosexual persons in our society and, often, the denial of their basic human rights.

At the same time, I have heard the rage and anguish of some Episcopalians who have felt disillusioned and confused about their homosexual sisters and brothers. They too want, with equal passion, to be given clear and unequivocal assurance that their beloved church is not disintegrating into the hedonism that our age seems to have spawned. For a number of people in our churches today many changes are not upsetting but frightening. They view the basic heterosexual relationship as so much a part of the natural order that it is fully normative. To hold that there can be other forms of God-given relationships raises difficult questions for them about the natural order and, therefore, even about the existence of God and God's purposes as they have understood them. They are also concerned that full acceptance of homosexual relationships would somehow mean a breakdown of all forms of sexual morality. I have sat with these people, too, and ached.

As your Presiding Bishop I need to share with you that the pain on both sides is real; neither side has cornered the market on anguish. I find that I share deeply in the pain and struggle of many individuals today and in the life of the church as we try to come to fuller understandings of human sexuality. I am hopeful that the pain and struggle can be redeemed and that they are leading us to both new compassion and vision. Compassion, if it is to be authentic, must be extended to all.

As Primate, Chief Pastor, and President, the titles given to me as Presiding Bishop, I am called to lead. But to lead does not mean to yank or to dictate. This is not the style of my ministry. Nor is it the mandate given me in our policy, in which I have neither the right nor the power to make unilateral declarations about such issues as who should or should not be ordained. Nor would I want such a prerogative. We Episcopalians proclaim the catholic faith; we strive to be a collegial church.

In a controversy, then, my leadership must consist of clarifying the issue and building bridges. It is the vision of wholeness—of the oneness that is ours in Christ—that I hope will lead me all the days of my ministry as Presiding Bishop. To be a bridge builder in a divided community is to reach out with *both* hands and to draw the sides together. This is the role of the prophetic pastor, seeking out both sides and enabling them to enter into dialogue for mutual understanding and acceptance.

To be a prophetic pastor is to live in tension—the tension of holding opposites together and the tension which grows out of deep compassion with those who have strong positions and passions. This is not a passive ministry but one of intentional engagement, constant growth and awareness, risk and vulnerability. I am called to this ministry and it is out of this that I can honestly say that there will be no outcasts.

In the midst of this long standing contention among us, what I yearn for is this: that we be honest and vulnerable in our sharing, compassionate in our listening, and diligent in our search for truth. In fact, I challenge the Episcopal Church with these tasks. I give you my pledge that I shall use all the resource and persuasion of my office to foster dialogue and study in the church on the matters of sexuality, homosexuality and relationships so that the myths can be dispelled, the prejudices overcome, the truth known, and our brokenness healed.

Letter to the House of Bishops, April 3, 1987

Many of you have written to me regarding the Church-wide discussion of human sexuality. Your letters tell me of your concern to create a constructive context in our Church while we come to our corporate mind as The Episcopal Church in matters of human sexuality. Many of you have shared with me letters and telephone calls you have received, as well as the questions put to you during your Episcopal visitations. My mail, too, indicates many are troubled and angry about things they have heard and read. I am writing to enlist you in actively exercising our roles as teachers and pastors at this important juncture in the process. I want to be helpful to you in continuing the process upon which we have embarked and, at the same time, be sensitive to the fear and anger that seems to be abroad in our Church over this issue.

Many have asked me to take a personal, public stand on such matters as blessing non-marital sexual relationships, including those of persons of the same sex—the issue that seems to have captured the headlines. I do not believe that at this time I should assume this responsibility, as the General Convention has asked its Standing Commission to bring to it a report and guidelines on such matters. I believe it is my role at this time to hold up for the whole Church a model of leadership which enables *any* subject to be discussed among us as long as such discussion is within a framework of mutual respect and loving kindness, which brings about a pastoral response. Discussion of sensitive issues can be painful for some since it may focus directly on behavior which has been traditionally unacceptable to the majority of the faithful. But, if we are not free as a family of God's people to engage one another in love and compassion, how are we being faithful to the Gospel we preach? No, it is my time to listen and to help us all to listen to one another. The Church will make its decisions soon enough.

The Church is not being asked to reject the Christian teaching on marriage and sexual intimacy. We must continue to uphold, affirm and do all that we can to support the life-long committed relationship of a woman and man as the ideal context for the expression of human sexual intimacy. This intimacy is a way of deepening relationships of care and love for one another and of providing the best setting for nurture. The Church's teaching has guarded against the moral, emotional and psychological chaos of a sexuality based solely on instinct or affection. Correctly understood, this position leads not to rejection and repression but true integration, since more is involved in sexual activity than pleasure.

The Christian sexual ethic is hard but it has been the experience of Christians that only when human love participates in something of the divine, unconditional love can the yearning of the human heart be satisfied. Many people do settle for relationships and sexual intimacy outside the Church's teaching. The question before us is how does the Church minister to those within or those outside the Christian community who engage in sexual intimacy outside the marriage state. . . . I believe we are hearing that there are many minds on this subject. What we must all strive for is the grace to hear God's voice in this discussion. Our responsibility is to be faithful to God's will, not merely bless the status quo.

From address to Episcopalians at the North American Congress on the Holy Spirit and World Evangelism, July 23, 1987

The question is how to live together as we explore the mystery of sexuality. We begin by lifting up the biblical and the theological. We proclaim that in our maleness and in our femaleness we mirror God's own life of complementary opposites. "God created man in the image of himself. In the image of God he created him, male and female he created them" (Genesis 1:27). Sexuality is close to God. I believe our human sexuality is a divine gift. Therefore, we treat all sexuality with care and with responsibility. Sex is important because God is important. That is why we in the Episcopal Church today are seeking to claim some time and attention for this issue.

Statement to the Episcopal Church, December 15, 1989

On Saturday, December 16, the bishop of Newark will ordain

to the priesthood a man who has acknowledged his homosexuality, who has lived for four years with another male, and who wishes to carry out a priestly ministry, particularly among the homosexual community. As this impending action is already receiving media attention, I felt that it was important that you be aware of facts related to the case and learn from me my thoughts on them.

In 1979, the General Convention passed a *resolution* that it is "not appropriate" to ordain practicing homosexual persons or any person engaging in heterosexual relationships outside of marriage. This still stands as "the mind of the House." In subsequent General Conventions efforts have been made to either strengthen this position—giving it the *canonical* force it does not now have—or to reverse it. Clearly, the General Convention is still in debate, and it is also "the mind of the House" that debate and dialogue on the topic of sexuality be continued.

It is my hope that the ordination in Newark will encourage positive debate, rather than polarization. It is my prayer that the debate will be conducted with respect and in an understanding that we are not talking about "us and them." We are one church family and are talking about how we will live together. . . .

In the midst of the controversy concerning this ordination in Newark, it is important to note that it is being carried out with the approval of the Commission on Ministry and the Standing Committee of the Diocese of Newark, as well as the bishop. . . .

As Presiding Bishop, I ask all members of the Episcopal Church to remember that we are not simply a political body in the business of passing resolutions; we are a church. As such, we understand the graceful action of God in our lives. We further understand that, through our baptism, we are all called to ministry and accountable to Jesus Christ. The ministry to which we are each called is not our ministry; it is the ministry of Jesus Christ.

Statement by the Presiding Bishop, joined by members of his Council of Advice, February 20, 1990

We feel called to address issues raised in the ordination by the Rt. Rev. John S. Spong of Newark on December 16, 1989, of Robert Williams, a homosexual person living in a public, avowed relationship with a person of the same sex.

Bishops are called to safeguard the unity of the church, a responsibility the Newark ordination has seemed to disregard. As the Presiding Bishop and Council of Advice, we disassociate ourselves from the action of the Standing Committee and Bishop of Newark in carrying out this ordination. We regret the hurt and confusion caused for many members of the church by the ordination and by subsequent events. Scandal within the church, whenever and however it may occur, is a profoundly serious matter. We believe that good order is not served when bishops, dioceses, or parishes act unilaterally. We believe that good order is served by adherence to the actions of General Convention.

We must stress here that our "disassociation" is not from the many members of our church who are gay and lesbian. Several conventions have affirmed and reaffirmed their God-given dignity, in common with all other members of the body of Christ. We do the same, and value their presence and their service within the church . . .

Responding to a case of clergy sexual misconduct: Address to Executive Council, November 10, 1992

I want to make a very strong point about (homosexuality and sexual misconduct). This particular case does involve homosexual behavior. But that is not what we are talking about here. We are talking about clergy sexual misconduct. That is what this case is all about. Sadly, priests of our church have also been deposed for sexual misconduct that was heterosexual in nature. We may be confident that had the victims in this case been female instead of male the offense would have been just as great and the church's disciplinary action would have been exactly the same.

The reason I am making such a point is that members of the gay and lesbian community—who are tired of being treated as issues anyway—don't want their sexuality to be discussed in the same conversation with sexual misconduct and the abuse of the pastoral relationship.

Sermon to Integrity Convention, July 10, 1992

And he took a child, and set him in the midst of them . . . Mark 9:36

. . . Christian journeying, growing up from your roots, has been on my mind lately . . . I spent a wonderful Independence Day weekend . . . with the youngest of my grandchildren, Joshua . . . Grandchildren are different. I do not recall feeling the same poignant feeling about my own children that grips my heart when I think about Joshua and his cousins. It's hard to explain. But when I look at him I feel as if I were handing over the world to him, as if I were placing it in his tiny hands as a gift. And mixed with my joy in giving him this gift is a feeling of dread, because I know what's in this world I'm handing over to Joshua, and he doesn't. He doesn't know about bigotry yet, for instance . . .

And I long—in a way that continues to surprise me—for Joshua's open-hearted surprise at the wonders his world unfolds before him to stay just the way it is. I long for him never to know cynicism. And so my joy in him is bittersweet, for he will know about cynicism—and war—and loneliness—and bigotry—and all those things we know about. He can't stay a child forever.

I was sitting outside watching him crawl around while I was thinking about what I'd say to you. I thought about your origins. I thought about what it has cost you to be honest about who you are. I thought about how accustomed you must have become to having people, who have never met you, form judgments about you based upon what you are rather than who you are. I guess you're used to it by now. But when I think about the years you spent getting used to it, I feel the same catch in my heart that I feel when I think about Joshua. I wish with all my heart that you had never had to get used to that. I wish you didn't have to know what you know. My grandson has never known what it feels like to be rejected and despised. I wish that you didn't know what it feels like, either. But I imagine that there is not a person in this room who has not been stung by it, and I know that there are some here who feel the sting today . . .

I am convinced that this church will never be reconciled about any issue unless we can reclaim the struggle in Christ's name with Christ's methods. I am convinced that neither side can win a war. Peace must break out. Reconciliation must begin. The struggle of Christ is not a project of seeing who can win. This is hard for a body like ours to grasp, since we do our business in the form of resolutions which are voted up or down, upon which we choose sides and lobby and caucus and win or lose. But we know that the legislative part of our common life as the Body of Christ is only one part. It's far from being the whole. When a resolution goes through, we know that this is not the end of the struggle. It is often only the beginning. The work of reconciliation is not completed in resolutions. It is spiritual work, and its tools are spiritual tools . . .

We are promised this reconciliation. It is the primary work of the church, the final fruit of Christ's saving death on the cross.

Sermon for the anniversary of Oasis, a gay ministry in New Jersey, June 4, 1996

. . . I must say that I am relieved to be able to stand here at a service commemorating the life of this compassionate and courageous organization, and not have to bear the burden of representing a church that views its own long standing practice of ordaining homosexual Christians as a violation of its doctrine! The outcome of the Righter presentment was both the one I expected and the one for which I hoped, and I know you felt the same. It is one step on a difficult path that we are walking in faith.

I was also heartened to read of the Supreme Court decision affirming the constitutional protection of the basic civil rights of gay and lesbian Americans, and I know you were, too. But, as I have said repeatedly, I now hope that those who do not greet these two legal events with satisfaction can, nonetheless, come to a different understanding of the place of litigation and legislation in a culture's spiritual and moral journey . . .

Never let anyone tell you that (the struggle of gay and lesbian Christians) is a "special interest." The struggle for human dignity is not a special interest. Christians are diminished when even one is objectified and marginalized. Gay and lesbian Christians are not a part of the division of the church, but a building block of its unity.

I read the scripture passage from today's gospel reading: "My prayer is not for them alone. I pray also for those who will believe in me through their message . . ." I thought of these two recent events, the Righter decision and the Supreme Court decision. I thought of this organization and its ministry of nurture and advocacy. I thought of those many, many persons who believe in Jesus, who have come to know the love of God, through the ministry of Oasis.

Oasis. The name is about shelter, about nurture, about drawing aside from the dusty and dangerous road for refreshment, for rest and cool water. The name "Oasis" speaks volumes about what the larger culture feels like to many gay and lesbian brothers and sisters: a desert, with no place to stop and rest, no one to offer that cool drink for which they long. Oasis. Come aside and be refreshed.

But an oasis is not just for rest and refreshment. You do not stay at the oasis in the desert. You rest and drink, and then you go your way again—back out into the difficult and dangerous desert. As precious a thing as it is to be, at last, in a place where you are safe, cared about and for, the purpose of the oasis is not itself. The purpose of the oasis is the journey. The oasis is part of the desert, its promise of the restoration of life and water to the parched earth, a green jewel in the midst of the hard clay and stinging sand.

The promise of this particular Oasis that we celebrate this evening embodies a promise for the whole Church, not just for its gay and lesbian members . . .

You have saved people's sanity and, in some cases, you have even saved people's lives. A community within the Church looks to you for comfort and challenge, and you do not disappoint that community. Living water is what you are. As you move into the future, remember that you are living water for everyone. Even for the ones who fear your witness, the ones who want nothing to do with you. Remember that the places most in need of living water are always the driest places, the places where you least want to be.

Wholesome Examples: Address to Executive Council, June 11, 1996

I honestly believe that one distant day our struggles around sexuality will be understood as having been essential in moving us closer to the heart of God. Having said that, let us recognize that they are not the focus of attention of the whole church. There are people out there, and you know them, who are simply sick to death of issues of sexuality so dominating the agenda.

The problem we experience is that these struggles get thrust to center stage through the overblown pronouncements of antagonists and protagonists of all points of view, and then magnified and distorted by the media of a culture that likes big and thinks simple. Jesus didn't give us his message in a cultural vacuum and his followers don't exist in one now. . . .

I have seen it my responsibility as Presiding Bishop to keep all parties at the table. That has been extraordinarily difficult. It would be far less complex to take up one position or another and advocate for it with all my might. Let me tell you I have been tempted. But this is not my ministry. However, I can say that I not only believe, I know, that it is possible for gay men and women in committed relationships to be wholesome examples. We see such examples every day. Let us remember here that Jesus said precious little about sexuality, and nothing specifically about homosexuality, being more concerned with hardness of heart. Would that we could turn our attention similarly.

I read the comment that for the past twenty years the most hotly debated issue in the Episcopal Church has been that of homosexuality. Tell that to a hungry child. Tell that to a single parent trying to hold the family together. Tell that to someone who fears for her life in an area of armed conflict.

Civil Rights: Statement on behalf of the Employment Non-Discrimination Act, July 19, 1995

On behalf of the Episcopal Church, I am proud and pleased to join with so many distinguished figures in the religious and civil rights communities in enthusiastic endorsement of S. 2238, the Employment Non-Discrimination Act of 1994. I offer my thanks to Senator Kennedy, an unwavering champion of civil rights for all Americans, for the opportunity to join with him today on behalf of this legislation. I am happy, also, to acknowledge the co-leading role of a devoted Episcopalian and good friend to our Church's public ministry, Senator Chafee, in bringing forth this landmark bill.

Since 1976, the Episcopal Church has been committed publicly to the notion of guaranteeing equal protection for all citizens, including homosexual persons, under the law. In that year, the General Convention of the Episcopal Church adopted Resolution A-71, expressing its conviction that homosexual persons are entitled to equal protection of the laws with all other citizens and calling upon society to ensure that such protection be provided in actuality. The Employment Non-Discrimination Act of 1994 explicitly fulfills the mandate, and I urge Members of Congress to move swiftly to pass the bill, and the President to sign it into law.

My warm embrace of this legislation, of course, reflects more than my standing as Presiding Bishop of the Episcopal Church. It represents my deep, personal belief in the intrinsic dignity of all God's children. The dignity demands that all citizens have a full and equal claim upon the promise of the American ideal, which includes equal civil rights protection against unfair employment discrimination. For far too long, our civil rights laws looked the other way with respect to discrimination based on race, gender, religion, national origin, age, and disability. Fighting to right those wrongs taught us that the cause of such protection for one is the cause of such protection for all. Today, so long as some of us remain subject to employment discrimination on the basis of sexual orientation, our system of civil rights protection for all Americans remains an unfulfilled ideal. The long overdue protection embodied in this legislation brings that ideal one significant step closer to reality.

Statement on gay and lesbian persons in the military, July 26, 1993

There are times when it would be easier to say nothing. This is one of those times. But I am moved to say that the "compromise" to allow gay and lesbian persons in the military deeply disappoints me and falls short of the compassion for which I had hoped. Let me say at the outset that this is a personal view. I do not attempt to speak for any other Episcopalian or even for the policy of our Church which supports equal protection under the law. And further let me say that I salute all those men and women, past and present, who have served our country in uniform.

But that salute includes those members of the military who are gay and lesbian. For me, the bottom line of the new policy is that it continues to discriminate against them. And that is wrong. We needed a policy that gave equal access and equal treatment to all persons in uniform. A military code of sexual conduct applied equally to homosexual and heterosexual personnel was the way to go. That was the charge President Clinton laid down.

We are a democracy and it is the role of the military to defend the values and principles of that democracy. But the military does not determine those values and principles. I think it was a mistake that this policy was developed solely within the military establishment and ignored Secretary Aspin's own civilian Rand report.

I commend the courage of President Clinton for taking on this issue. He had it right the first time. This was a moral and civil rights matter of equal protection under the law. Bigotry, ignorance and fear have no place in the formulation of our nation's policies. Our values of fairness and tolerance are sound values deserving of protection not only by our military but within it.

AIDS

When Bishop Browning came into office, the issue of HIV/AIDS was contentious in the church. Some members believed the disease was punishment for immoral behavior. From the moment of his election, Browning came out strongly in support of a pastoral response by the church to

this pandemic. By the next General Convention in Detroit in 1988, the Episcopal Church had developed a wide ministry of caring and concern. Detroit featured a display of the AIDS quilt and Browning led a healing service.

In 1988 he invited each bishop to develop a pastoral relationship with a person with AIDS. Browning led the way by example, regularly visiting an AIDS patient until his death.

In December, 1989, Browning disassociated himself from the ordination of Robert Williams, a gay man in relationship with a male partner, because he viewed the ordination as a breach of an agreement among the bishops. However, when Williams lay dying from AIDS two years later Browning made a death bed visit to see him. The visit was never reported.

On October 11, 1996, Browning celebrated a Eucharist at the National Episcopal AIDS Coalition gathering in Washington D.C. This was set in the context of the display of The NAMES Project AIDS Memorial Quilt. Forty thousand panels, containing 70,000 names of persons who have died from AIDS, covered the entire mall from the monument to the Capitol. Browning was one of ten national sponsors of the event which included President Clinton. He spent time viewing the Quilt and when asked how he felt, remarked that he was deeply touched and like most observers, shed a few tears. Later, he joined Pamela Chinnis, president of the House of Deputies, in a public reading of names of the dead.

His presence at that event and his willingness to identify himself completely with the pain and hurt of those affected by the disease was a poignant moment which captured the true compassion of the man.

Acceptance Speech, September 12, 1985

I wish to express my pleasure at the action of this Convention in its compassionate response to persons with AIDS. And I assure you that I will fulfill those portions of the resolution asked of the Presiding Bishop.

House of Bishops, San Antonio, September 22, 1986

The issue of AIDS is a good example of how, out of its pastoral life, the Church raises an issue for national attention and leads the body politic in addressing the needs of those persons afflicted. Important to the well-being of our society as any is the issue of AIDS—the last General Convention was clear in its direction. The tragedy increases—the suffering is incredible as it reaches into all segments of our society—and every indication is that much of society as well as our government has lacked the compassion to reach out and make a difference. Even parts of the religious community have issued judgments that can only increase the myths and phobias to the point of demeaning.

There are a lot of questions—the question of the dignity of life and the dignity of death—the question of hope—the question of accountability—the question of collective health for all people—the question of the cost of research—how will the burden be borne? No one questions the research of cancer—would it not be tragic if the cancer patient was expected to pay the whole cost?

We have set as our goals: to help the Church in its pastoral outreach to those suffering from AIDS, their friends and families; to provide materials and resources for the needed consciousness awakening; and finally, to take an advocacy role in Washington for a greater commitment to research.

Statement on AIDS, November 1986

The 68th General Convention requested that the Presiding Bishop "establish and lead a National Day of Prayer and Healing with special intentions for the AIDS crisis." This request was in the "Love and compassion (for) the tragic human suffering and loss of life involved in the AIDS epidemic . . ." Responding to both the General Convention's intention and to the pastoral and spiritual dimensions of this deepening health and social issue, I ask all Episcopalians to join me on Sunday, November 9, 1986, in offering prayers and intercessions for people with AIDS and for those who minister to them . . .

The Christian community can offer care and compassion, resources and reconciliation, hospitality and hope. Above all, we can provide for some of the spiritual and pastoral needs of people with AIDS and those who share their suffering. We can be a fountain of ever-flowing love and a foundation for a community of grace.

"And the king will answer, 'I tell you this: anything you did for one of my brothers here, however humble, you did for me'." (Matthew 24:40)

Letter on AIDS, September 10, 1987

I am now reading their names nearly every morning on the obituary page of the newspaper. Sometimes there is a photo with a young, bright face looking out at me. The words are always similar: "died after a long illness . . . surviving are mother and father." More often, now, the account of death is more honest and explicit: "died due to AIDS related complications." I read this in cities across the country—Charlotte, North Carolina; Evansville, Illinois; St. Louis. And, I read it in cities overseas—Geneva, London and Osaka. Persons living with AIDS are from a wide spectrum of society: bankers, artists, teachers, clergy and even the founder of a conservative political action group. The recurring accounts of newborn children with AIDS strikes a deep chord of empathy as well as grief.

The suffering of each of these persons physically, mentally and spiritually is incalculable. The personal search for a cure or relief is often frantic and ultimately fruitless and costly. Parents and friends react in varying degrees of horror, panic, fear and shame. Some rise to heroic compassion and service. The physical pain is joined by social ostracism and the politicization of the condition. The agony of the person living with AIDS, family, friends and loved ones, goes beyond dispassionate telling.

No matter how deep and traumatic may be the suffering of persons living with AIDS, we cannot measure the anguish of those countless millions in high risk groups who are living with the fear of AIDS. The five or more years incubation period of the disease-causing virus leaves these millions caught in a wasteland of fear and guilt. Every rash is potentially Kaposi's sarcoma. Every cold is pneumocystis carinii pneumonia. And how do you answer the not-too-subtle questions on life and medical insurance forms? Or, what will be the response to the "routine" medical examination for that new job?

For the homosexual person, the closet may be a living hell. However, for some it may be the only way to survive in a hostile community. For these people, who don't confront others, don't blab about their private lives, who just hope people will leave them alone, these, too, are the people living with AIDS.

Message on AIDS, October 1987

For Christians, AIDS challenges the heart of our faith. Because AIDS is ruthless and indiscriminate, it confronts us with the oldest and hardest paradox: how can an all-loving God permit this plague? Or worse, we ask: Is this what God wills? Why does the Lord not intervene? Can our loving God really want an infant to suffer and die from AIDS? Or hemophilia? Can a truly all-merciful deity stand by and watch any child suffer so?

It is hard not to be spiritually shaken in the face of these questions. It is so much easier to focus on fighting AIDS on scientific, secular turf, or on supposedly moral grounds, to blame its victims.

And so it is that AIDS provides us with a prodigious spiritual challenge. For I am persuaded that, in the midst of the anguish of AIDS—in the very center of it—we are being called home to the basic tenets of our faith. While it is not easy to see grace in so dreadful a situation as this, I believe God's light can shine forth with unprecedented radiance precisely by virtue of this excruciating chapter in world history. I believe we are being called anew to trust in God and to be willing to help and suffer with others. I call for compassion. . . .

We simply cannot know why this disease has erupted into human history. And we dare not be so arrogant as to claim this as God's judgment on anyone. All we can affirm is that God's wisdom is not our wisdom and that it is for God alone to judge. We are left with only one viable option: to trust in God's care for the creation and God's strong purpose of redemption even in all of this, to throw ourselves on the Lord's mercy and to trust—when all reason fails us—that God is loving us even now, even as those we love are dying. We must remember that we worship and trust a God who became incarnate, who was an outcast, who suffered, who overcame death.

Letter to the Episcopal Church, October 1991

In the aftermath of the Persian Gulf War, I continue to wonder at the power, might, and resources that were brought to bear on that fragile region of the world. I am struck, in contrast, at our often halfhearted response to the pain and tragedy of our society, especially the tragedy of HIV/AIDS.

Let me share a concrete illustration of the effects of HIV/AIDS in the United States alone. If we were to erect a memorial to the AIDS dead of this country, it would need to be of equal length but twice the height of the Vietnam War Memorial to accommodate all of the names of those who have died of AIDS. And sadly, the conflict with HIV/AIDS has not ended. . . .

We must sustain our commitment and increase our efforts. We Episcopalians must not be content with the notion that it is now possible for people living with HIV/AIDS to live longer.

We must pray and work together for the long haul. The call is for ongoing, substantive research that seeks a cure to this scourge, which elicits both the very best and the worst from us. . . .

May God strengthen and provide, heal and console, guide and focus our hearts and minds and give us courage to remain faithful and steadfast to the Gospel's lead.

One World, One Hope, a statement released October 1, 1996

. . . We acknowledge and give thanks for the hope now breaking forth for those living with HIV/AIDS through new treatments, but we must confess that economic injustice and racism will make this hope stillborn for tens of millions in our own nation, and for most in the developing world . . .

I ask you to re-double your efforts for justice as we can no longer overlook or remain blind to the link between AIDS and poverty, AIDS and racism, and AIDS and human oppression.

And I ask you to help save the lives of our children and our children's children by giving them life-saving AIDS prevention information, and educating them in the Christian values of wholeness, love, and acceptance.

Our hope is in Christ who called all people to himself and made them whole. Our world is not defined by geographic boundaries, but by the fullness of God's love, through whom no one is forgotten or neglected. One World. One Hope. Let this be our clarion call, and the focus of our commitment to prayer for all who suffer due to HIV and AIDS.

RACISM

In the manner of John Hines, Edmond Browning spoke out many times against the evil of racism from the beginning to the end of his tenure as Presiding Bishop.

Three events particularly sparked his passion on this issue. First, when Arizona voters overturned a law to recognize Martin Luther King Day, Browning directed his energies toward launching a major initiative against racism during and beyond the 1991 General Convention in Phoenix. Browning, among other actions, participated in a march in Phoenix in support of a Martin Luther King Day in January, 1991, seven months before the convention.

Second, Browning was deeply affected by the Los Angeles riots in the wake of the Rodney King verdict in the spring of 1992. He flew immediately to Los Angeles to visit affected congregations.

Third, he was touched by the plight of American Indians after visiting Episcopal ministries on reservations. He launched a vigorous program of self determination by creating a separate council on Indian ministries made up solely of Episcopal Indians.

A specific event is worth mentioning. Twice during his term, Congress threatened to open the Arctic National Wildlife Refuge to oil exploration. The Gwich'in Indians who live in the refuge are virtually all members of the Episcopal Church and Browning acted as their advocate. The White House and members of Congress were impressed by the Episcopal Church's presence in ANWR and it's national church's commitment to protecting them. Oil exploration would have scattered the caribou herds on which the Gwich'in depend. One White House source told the church's government relations director that it was the Episcopal Church's compelling advocacy that persuaded President Clinton to promise a veto of any bill that would threaten the refuge. ANWR remains protected today.

The slave trade: Address to the Interim House of Bishops, San Antonio, September 21, 1986

On February 23, 1807, the British House of Commons declared the slave trade illegal and forbade any participation by British merchants in the sale and transportation of slaves. This victory over one of humanity's greatest evils was in no small part due to William Wilberforce, an evangelical who became the leader of the anti-slavery movement. Wilberforce and his companions formed a group of serious-minded church people, mostly of considerable wealth and position, at the Church of the Holy Trinity, Clapham. The so-called "Clapham Sect" were devoted to the Church and committed their money, their influence and their ability in support of the missionary outreach of the Church and, with the maturity of the movement, to a deep sense of social responsibility and to the needs of the weak, the ignorant and the exploited. In the eyes of the Evangelicals, there was nothing more offensive than the slave trade. And, with Wilberforce in the lead, they were relentless in pressing the government to outlaw the exploitation of human beings.

Every year over 100,000 slaves were transported from Africa to America. It has been calculated that of the approximately twenty million Africans transported to the British West Indies, only 20 percent survived the sea voyage. The slave trade was profitable, bringing labor to the cotton, sugar and tobacco plantations and cheap raw materials to the English mills. The slave trade was supported by many powerful groups in England—merchants, shippers and planters. The English mills were dependent upon it, as were the West Indian plantations. Many in England turned a blind eye to the evils of the system and comforted themselves with the thought of British prosperity and progress. Against the "vested interests" and the inertia and complacency of public opinion stood the Evangelicals. They had only one weapon with which to fight—and that was righteousness, the appeal to conscience. In his *History of the*

English Speaking People, Winston Churchill called Wilberforce the conscience of the Parliament and the Prime Minister. The success of Wilberforce, after eighteen years of struggle, shows what religious and moral conviction can do even against the heaviest odds.

At the end of a three-and-a half hour speech in the House of Commons in 1789, Wilberforce cried: "Sir, when we think of eternity and of the future consequences of all human conduct, what is there in this life that should make any man contradict the dictates of his conscience, the principles of justice and the laws of God?"

In 1833, one month after Wilberforce's death, all slavery was abolished throughout the British dominions. Out of a study of the Bible, private prayer and devotion, public worship and the highest sense of public morality, Wilberforce and the Evangelicals defeated the combined forces of slavery. They provide us with a model for social conscience and action.

Institutional racism: Remarks to Executive Council, November 1986

I want to share with you this morning that I have a sense coming out of what I have experienced in the last ten months that no greater challenge faces the Church than that of racism. In my sermon at the recent meeting of the House of Bishops, I shared my growing awareness that we must not be tricked to think that the struggle of apartheid is limited to South Africa. The struggle is with the pernicious evil of institutional racism. The greater question before us is not, necessarily, how we support the anti-apartheid forces in South Africa, but how will we confront the racism that pervades all human society? Are we prepared to work for a United States and a world where all people of every color are enabled to play an equal part? . . . The struggle against racism is dramatically engaged in South Africa, no question about it, but it is being fought around the world: in the

Middle East, Southeast Asia, in Sri Lanka, Central America, and, as we know, even in many parts of this country.

The issue of institutional racism keeps coming forward as I travel and as I meet with church people in this country and representatives from abroad. When I met with the national leadership of the National Commission on Indian Work and other representatives of the Native American community, the issue of racism was one of their greatest concerns. When I met with members of the representatives of the Hispanic community in the Southwest, the issue was racism. When I met on several different occasions with the Union of Black Episcopalians, the issue was racism. I am sure that when I meet with the leadership of the Asian-American community the issue will be the same. The issue is racism and often that issue is translated into different means: quality education, medical care, employment, housing, and social services.

In the Episcopal Church we must practice what we preach and teach. Indeed, there is no more effective way of preaching and teaching. We must find more effective ways for the Episcopal Church to influence public policy regarding institutional racism through the force of our own example and the credibility of the teaching process itself. I was struck by a recent interview in The New York Times, with the Roman Catholic Auxiliary Bishop of Brooklyn. Bishop Joseph M. Sullivan said: "The major problem the church has is internal. How do we teach? As much as I think we're responsible for advocating public issues, our primary responsibility is to teach our own people. We haven't done that. We're asking politicians to do what we haven't done effectively ourselves." I cannot agree more with that statement. . . .

It would be precipitous for me to establish unilaterally a program and agenda to address institutional racism. I do think that it is appropriate for me to state that this is a priority for the months ahead.

Statement on the Arizona referendum, General Convention, November 14, 1990

The Episcopal Church will go to Phoenix. The business of the church is to witness to the Gospel, and that is exactly what we will do in Arizona. As Dr. King himself said, "The church must be reminded that it is not the master or servant of the state, but rather the conscience of the state . . ." We are called to be that conscience, and we accept that call.

I am well aware that the National Football League has decided it will express its disapproval of the referendum by choosing not to go to Arizona. We do not have that choice. We are in this for the long haul. We cannot turn our backs on the injustice dealt to minorities, including our Native American brothers and sisters in the Diocese of Navajoland who have long looked upon our coming to Arizona as an opportunity to lift up their special concerns.

There are people of good faith in Arizona who are working and fighting to overcome prejudice. The fight has been a very bruising one, and they need our support. I have today talked to a number of African-Americans in Arizona, who have assured me that our presence would strengthen their cause. We will therefore stand with them and together make a vigorous witness for the dignity of all God's people. We are now in the very early stages of planning a witness against racism that will permeate the entire fabric of our convention. Our convention theme, "Seek and Serve Christ in All Creation," is a reminder to us of why we need to be in Arizona. We are called to make this witness there because it is our General Convention site. However, we must not, in a spirit of self-righteousness, point fingers at any one part of our nation. Racism is a sickness that afflicts our entire society.

Plans at this time call for our witness to begin on the King holiday in January when I will go to Phoenix and honor the memory of Dr. King and his vision of a nonracist society. The city of Phoenix has an active celebration of that day, and members of our church will take part in it . . .

When I visited with members of the Arizona legislature last winter to support the passage of the successful bill on the King holiday, I said that I was not issuing threats about not coming to Arizona. I went on to say that I believed that they were confronting a moral issue of deep significance. Dr. King had a dream of what this country could be if we were able to find racial equality. Observing a holiday in his name goes beyond honoring him and reminds us of his vision. It reminds us of who we are called to be as God's people.

We will go to Arizona and live the dream.

Statement on the Los Angeles riots, May 1, 1992

As a nation we watched with horror and shame the video image of the beating of Rodney King by public servants bound to protect us all. With outrage we received news of the acquittal of those responsible, and asked what this says about our judicial system. Now, we must confront the further horror of violence unleashed—as despair and frustration are vented and meaninglessness takes a brutal form. And we must ask if this is what happens when a society does not govern itself guided by an inner conviction that every person is of equal value.

The events in Los Angeles—the brutal beating, the acquittal, the equally brutal misplaced response—have given us a chilling reminder that racism is rampant in our midst. We have dismal fresh evidence of our capacity for sin and evil. Though this is not new information, it compels us to confess that in the twenty-five years between the hopeful dream of Martin King and the hopeless nightmare of Rodney King we as a nation have made little moral progress.

The violent events in Los Angeles and in other cities of our nation are a reminder that, as the Kerner Commission reported in the 1960's, we are two nations—separate and unequal. The time for dimensioning the nature of the problem is past. We must act.

At our General Convention in Phoenix this past summer, I committed myself and our church to the elimination of the sin of racism. We adopted resolutions binding ourselves to work toward that reality, within and outside our structure. In these tense and difficult days, I call on each of you to recommit yourself to your baptismal vows, and ask for your prayers and efforts toward healing, understanding, and tolerance. As a beginning, I ask that you join with others on Sunday, May 3, in a Day of Prayer for Racial Justice.

This church is committed to the eradication of racism.

Letter to an Episcopal layman, May 20, 1992

I want to say at the outset how much I appreciate your thoughtful letter of May 4. It was very good of you to take the time to write. The Episcopal Church is very blessed to have people such as yourself to help us struggle with the hard issues of our day.

Your comments critical of certain parts of my open statement are helpful. In response, I determined that I needed to make a pastoral statement that would reach the anguished cry of members of this Church to help vent some of their anger and distress. Most of those persons are people of color who belong to congregations in our urban areas, including affected congregations in Los Angeles. Those persons share a different perspective than yours of the events surrounding the beating of Rodney King and the acquittal of four police officers.

Emotions are high on this issue and I wish you could have been with me to see the anguish of our members in those affected congregations in Los Angeles. Our task now is to enter into a very serious dialogue between those persons and the rest of the Church. Right now, those good Church people in south central Los Angeles do not have the luxury to see events in the dispassionate way you do. Your comments reflect the chasm that exists between members of our own Church on this very difficult and serious issue.

My hope is to bring good persons like yourself together with others in this Church so that we may be about the task of rooting out racism not only in our society, but within the structures of the Church itself.

Of community and the contrite heart: Column in *Episcopal Life*, June 1992

While smoke still hung over a battered City of the Angels, the faithful gathered in churches around our nation to grieve and to pray. In the Church of St. Mary in the wounded Koreatown section of Los Angeles, I joined with sisters and brothers of the diocese to break bread, to pray, and to offer one another the comfort of our common grief . . .

All through Eastertide we have remembered and celebrated how Christ's sacrifice and God's love transformed the cross of presumed defeat into the symbol of victory. Transformation is the way of Christ, beginning with each of us. We are each challenged to conversion of the heart. It won't do to say that we were not there when it happened. We were there. We were there when they crucified our Lord, and we were there when Rodney King was beaten and Los Angeles was set ablaze. We were there when a child was taught to hate and a young person was made to feel shame because of the color of his skin or the shape of her eyes. We were all there.

This is what it means to belong to one another. The service at St. Mary's was a sacramental reminder for me of what Christian community is. We came together, bonded by our love of Christ, our unity through our baptism, and our desire to be faithful to the demands of discipleship. We came to the Lord's table for comfort, and acknowledged our need for strength as well. God knows we need that strength.

We sang on that sad day in Los Angeles. We sang of the judgment of that day and all days. We sang of our Lord's waiting upon us, though we spurn him. Though we fail and falter,

Christ is faithful. He continues to offer peace from the hill of Calvary. There is hope. We know that, through our pain and our shame. Men and women—gathered to pray, grieving for Los Angeles, grieving as well for all the ways and places where the sin of racism makes us less than we are meant to be . . .

Over the last days I have frequently heard the disturbances in our cities referred to as a "wake-up call" to our divided nation. I hope so. Too long have we slumbered.

The sin of racism: Address to Executive Council, Albuquerque, June 16, 1992

. . .We have been led by God's Spirit for some time to put the eradication of racism at the top of our agenda. If we hadn't known this before the Arizona legislature failed to declare a paid Martin Luther King state holiday in 1990 and all hell broke loose, we certainly knew it then. We committed ourselves to an intense effort against racism in Phoenix, and the General Convention set our course. It did not take the fires of Los Angeles to illuminate this for us. Those grim days in urban areas of our nation only affirmed that, whatever our efforts, they are desperately needed. They showed us that the task is great, and the time is now, as tensions went from simmer to boil.

As most of you know, I went to Los Angeles in the days immediately following the outbreak of violence to stand in solidarity with the people there on behalf of the whole church. The time meant a great deal to me, though it was not an easy time. It was extraordinarily painful to talk with people who had lost all they had, who were afraid, perhaps whose homes were intact but whose souls were deeply wounded. There were deep wounds to all races and pain enough for everyone.

I also saw how we, the church at our best, can begin to rise to the occasion. I saw grief and horror transformed by human caring and compassion. It was another time in my life when I have been called to reflect that out of every tragedy comes an opportunity for revisioning, for transformation. That is the lesson of the Cross.

I am returning to California this weekend to . . . go to Compton, a community that is 98 percent black and that has suffered great devastation and deep wounding. It is very clear to me that the church must make a continuing witness of our solidarity with those who struggle to rebuild, to heal the wounds and to be instruments of transformation . . .

I know sin when I see it. [Racism] is sin. Let us not shrink from naming it for what it is. This is deep sin that was bred in greed and leads to violence, to the death of hope, of dreams, and to tragic waste of human potential.

We cannot set ourselves apart from this. It does no good to say that you or I or our neighbor is "not personally involved." How can we not be involved when we are part of a society—and let me say it—a privileged and empowered part of a society that tolerates the existence of a permanent underclass in our midst? We are involved.

How can we say we are not involved when that same society of which we are a part not only allows but facilitates the holding on to privilege and abuse of power by white people at a bitter cost to everyone else? We are involved.

How can we say we are not involved when within the structures of our own church we find subtle and not so subtle indications of the racism that infests our own society? Our racism audit (begun by action of the Phoenix General Convention) gave us a way to begin working on that, and I pray God we have the strength and the humility to confront our own sin.

Surely, surely as people saved by the redeeming love of Jesus we know not only what sin is, we know what repentance is. We know what it is to fall to our knees, to ask for forgiveness and for healing. As we look to be agents of change, of transformation, we must each begin in our own heart . . .

As we work, we must keep in mind a holistic vision of our

battle against racism because it is not an isolated issue. It is tightly bound up with other social, economic and environmental issues. If, for example, the Environmental Stewardship Team, appointed after General Convention, does not see that it has a role to play in addressing racial issues, then we will be a divided church. If our outreach in this Decade of Evangelism is disconnected from our efforts against racism, we are losing the moment.

All of the churches are working on initiatives against racism, and we have agreed that we must work more ecumenically. Groups within our church need to cooperate as well. I applaud the Episcopal Urban Caucus for their seven-point program and am grateful to the Union of Black Episcopalians for their prodding and keeping the issue before us. I welcome that challenge and encourage other groups to challenge and sensitize us to their concerns. . . .

I believe the church has a major role to play in this and we are in it for the long haul. There is no quick fix or simple solution to problems that have plagued humankind since the fall. There are just a lot of small, difficult steps over a hilly and winding path. We can't make the journey all at once. We have to be accountable every day. By "we" I mean each and all of us, corporately and as individuals before our maker. We have to keep asking the deep questions and being the church every day. We have to keep asking what we can do—in our homes, our communities, our churches and everywhere we find ourselves. We have to keep asking what we can do, and praying for the strength to do it. The task is enormous—but the power of God is truly unlimited.

Speech to Episcopal Charities, May 25, 1995

The context for our mission as a Church is always changing. The Oklahoma bombing has given us a wake-up call much as the LA riots did several years ago. In Los Angeles, we learned that racism still has deep roots in our society despite the progress we have made since the days of segregation. Our Church has taken on the issue of racism diocese by diocese, congregation by congregation, but not without a lot of resistance which continues today. I continue to call upon every Episcopalian to engage this issue, for we shall never be well until we have rooted racism out of the soul of this Church.

The Oklahoma bombing is also a wake-up call. And it is not unrelated to racism. Oklahoma is confirmation that hate is a part of American society today. It is expressed in shocking ways on radio stations throughout the country. We see armed militias threatening the Federal government. But make no mistake. These voices of hate and wicked violence are sown by extremist groups which promote neo-nazism, racism, anti-semitism, Japan-bashing and branding all Arabs as terrorists. They give license to street gangs to beat up and murder innocent people for the crime of being gay.

These forces of hate are not new. But we are only now waking up to the threat they make to the social fabric of our country. Americans like to think of themselves as fair and sympathetic to the needs of the least among us. What we are seeing now is that America is engaged in a struggle to preserve its liberties and respect for diversity among peoples.

AMERICAN INDIANS

A message of hope: Address to Executive Council, South Dakota, May, 1988

This week you and I have witnessed how hopelessness ravages the human body, soul and spirit as we visited the Reservation. Wounded Knee is a dramatic monument not only to an historic event of inhumanity, it is constant testimony to injustice that continues to this day. Wounded Knee is the place of the wounded human spirit. It is a place where one is forced to meditate on the robbery not only of life, of land, of culture, of dignity, but of hope! What is the message of hope that we bring to Native Americans?

What do we say to the Native Americans of South Dakota, who are living in nine of the nation's poorest counties? What is the message of hope? What do we say to 80 percent of the Native Americans on the reservation who are unemployed? What do we say to the Native Americans living with the complications of diabetes, the incidence of which is 10 to 15 times greater than the national average? What do we say to the Native Americans whose sacred land is being violated for profit, who are harassed when they exercise their lawful fishing and hunting rights? What do we say to the family of William Wainanwit, who at 25 years old drank himself into a stupor one day, went out behind the family trailer and hanged himself? What is the message of hope? . . .

How do we develop an intentionality in response to the physical and spiritual crisis we have all witnessed this week? And, how do we ensure partnership of Native communications in shaping that intentionality? What do we need to do that we ought to be doing? What is the message of hope that we Episcopalians have to share?

One of the first things that I did when I came to the Office of the Presiding Bishop was to name a Blue Ribbon Task Force on Indian Affairs. I charged this small task force with advising me on pending legislative issues touching on Native Americans. I propose now to expand that Blue Ribbon Task Force and charge this body with bringing to the Church recommendations on what we ought to be doing, and how to do it.

To honor our commitment to partnership with Indian people in the full life and ministry of this Church, I plan to have Native

Americans comprise at least 75 percent of the members of this expanded task force.

I charge this task force with helping our Church to respond to the spiritual needs of Indian people, on how we can fulfill our commitment to share the Gospel of Jesus Christ with Indian people. Ninty-two percent of American Indians do not go to church. Some of our priests serving Native congregations serve 10 congregations. Are current models of ministry viable with Native Americans? For instance, is the non-stipendiary clergy concept appropriate when unemployment rates run so high on the reservation?

I charge this task force with helping our Church to respond to the violations of treaty rights. I charge this task force with helping our Church to combat racism as it uniquely effects Native Americans. I charge this task force with helping our Church construct a comprehensive model for funding of Indian ministries.

The message of hope to Native Americans is not found in returning to paternalism, or ecclesiastical colonialism or cultural imperialism. The message of hope to Native Americans is not found in Band-Aid approaches. The message of hope to Native Americans is not carried out in pious words, unrealistic promises, or here-today-gone-tomorrow friendship.

The message of hope that we bring to our Native American sisters and brothers is that we have heard loud and clear their appeal for real involvement in the decisions that effect their lives as Episcopalians. We have heard their call for Indian partnership, for Indian empowerment in the policy decision-making in this Church. The National Committee on Indian Work has been restructured and revitalized, new ministry has begun in the urban communities, where half of the Indian population now reside, new models of ministry are being developed. The message that I want to give in this place is that this work must be carried forward and I will see it through.

The message that I want to leave with our Native American leadership is that through Jesus Christ we are one. Through Jesus Christ we are partners in a community of grace. Through Jesus Christ we find God at work in our lives. Through Jesus Christ we have HOPE. Through Jesus Christ we have new life.

Toward a new partnership: Remarks to Coalition, February 14, 1990

I spent the early part of my tenure as your Presiding Bishop in a "listening" process and it was a short 10 months after I took office that I participated in the second of two consultations which were jointly sponsored by Coalition 14 and the National Committee on Indian Work.

This second consultation on Indian ministry was called Oklahoma II, and it was held in October, 1986, in Oklahoma City. A paper came out of that consultation called "Covenant of Oklahoma II." It identified seven action items deemed necessary to fulfill the Anglican/Episcopal Church's early commitment—a commitment that goes back to the first permanent English settlement on this continent—to bring the Gospel of Jesus Christ to the peoples of these shores.

Spoken to in the Oklahoma Covenant was racism, empowerment of native peoples, cross-cultural understanding, indigenous leader training—both lay and ordained—curricula, and exposure of the whole church to native spirituality.

Until this point we've not progressed a lot on the specific call which was issued at Oklahoma II for "exploration and experimentation within the very near future, alternative modes of Church governance and structure."

Each time I visited Indian country, I pondered again and again: What is it we're not doing, that we ought to be doing? How do we develop a programmatic response to the human suffering . . . the spiritual crisis . . . in Indian Country? How do we call our nation and our government to honor its treaty obligations? How do we endure partnership of Native communicants?

Early in my tenure—in fact I believe it was within a month after I took office—I appointed a Blue Ribbon Task Force on Indian Affairs to advise me on legislative issues affecting American Indians. That task force recommended that we focus on Indian Health, and we finally got the Indian Health Reauthorization Bill passed and signed by the President—it had been vetoed once.

It was when I went with Executive Council to Rapid City, S.D., and visited the Pine Ridge Reservation, that it became even more clear to me that "there are things that this Church is not doing that it ought to be doing" among the native peoples of this country . . . The day before, I had stood on a windswept hill of a prairie, a place known as Wounded Knee, a place of pain and sorrow, site of that appalling slaughter 100 years ago this December.

A Choctaw priest, Steven Charleston, gave a morning meditation, there in Rapid City . . . Steve said, "The Episcopal Church has an extraordinary opportunity. Very strong leadership is now in place. You must, however, trust native leadership. Let it go. You'll be a little scared, but let it go. Let it go."

It was there, at Rapid City, S.D., that I announced to the Executive Council my plan to expand the Blue Ribbon Task Force, and I charged them with telling me what we ought to be doing, and how to do it . . . The task force recommended a new configuration which would see a confluence of National Committee on Indian Work and that part of Coalition 14 which responds to funding needs for Native American ministry. The task force stressed that this new entity—to be called Episcopal Council of Indian Ministries—is necessary to provide a coordinated, visible, ongoing, and focused structure for the accomplishment of Indian work and ministry.

I just want to leave you with these thoughts. Transitions are a time of tension and potential polarity. At times there are extended desert experiences in the transition. There are questions of vision and direction, the necessity to feed the hungry, to form the leadership and motivate and unite the community.

The Episcopal Church is now in a period of transition, a time of new partnerships in mission.

'Discovery' translates racism: Statement for 500th anniversary of Columbus' arrival in the Americas, October 12, 1992

I am heartened to see the Episcopal Church joining many others to question a "celebration" for the 500th anniversary of the "discovery of the Americas."

The perception that the Americas were discovered only 500 years ago renders the American Indian invisible in the consciousness of our nation. Every effort must be made to remind our nation of the rich heritage of this country's true forebears, the Indians.

The focus on the 500th anniversary of "Columbus' discovery" unveils a deep disquiet within me because I see within it the ugly specter of racism. I fear for this racism and triumphalism that lurks so predominately behind the plans for celebrating Columbus' "discovery." Looking deeply into our past we will see not only the cruel and unjust fate of the American Indian, but the consequences on other peoples of color who came to this land, many against their will. From black people brought in slavery, to the gross mistreatment of Asians who migrated to the North American continent, we see a pattern of violence, abuse, and genocide.

Our Church is struggling to face up to the racism that remains deeply imbedded in our national life and, yes, even in the Church's. While many rightly champion gains that have been made, we still are far short of the vision of a nation that lives out its creed that all are created equal.

For those whose roots come from the shores of Europe, the 500th anniversary of Columbus' arrival is an opportunity for reflection and repentance. And from such reflection we may then be moved to celebrate instead the diversity of our nation among its peoples and cultures.

Let the Church lead, as it should, on this issue. Our claim as a people of faith is to lift up the blessings of God from every corner of Creation. My hope is that alternative celebrations of the survival and spirit of our native peoples can be occasion for advances against the sin of racism and move us on toward the vision of the reign of God.

The Gwich'in: Letter to Senators Al Gore, Max Baucus, Joseph Lieberman, Bennett Johnston, June 21, 1991

I write you today about a matter of intense personal concern to the Episcopal Church in the United States, of which I am Presiding Bishop.

The Gwich'in Athabascan Indians, who live in the Arctic, are involved in a struggle for their survival. All of the Gwich'in are members of the Episcopal Church.

I want to thank you for your work to oppose legislation before Congress that would open the Arctic National Wildlife Reserve to oil exploration. Let me be clear that the national Episcopal Church stands four-square with our Gwich'in brothers and sisters in opposing this legislation.

The Gwich'in have developed their life and culture for 10,000 years. Oil development of their homeland threatens to end this way of life. The primary concern is that the Caribou, the prime source of livelihood for the Gwich'in, would be displaced by oil drilling, driving the herds away from traditional calving grounds. Without the Caribou, the Gwich'in way of life would die.

Our government can and must do better by the Gwich'in. I encourage your support of energy legislation through conservation and safe alternative sources of energy.

III
PLACES

SOUTH AFRICA

Nowhere was the issue of racism more evident than in apartheid South Africa. In an address to Executive Council in June, 1989, the Presiding Bishop quoted Dorothy Soelle who said "Apartheid is not just a political system in an African country; apartheid is a certain way of thinking, feeling, and living without being conscious of what is happening around us." In response, Browning noted, "In this sense, none of us has to live in South Africa to be a victim of apartheid."

The Episcopal Church was always a leader in the anti-apartheid movement, and was the first church to file a shareholder resolution in 1971 with General Motors. This launched a 20-year campaign of various economic sanctions against South Africa. Bishop Browning picked up where his predecessors left off as soon as he was elected Presiding Bishop, referring to apartheid in his acceptance speech and maintaining unwavering support for the South African Anglican church in the long and ultimately successful campaign to end apartheid.

Browning made several trips to South Africa during his tenure as a means of expressing his solidarity with Desmond Tutu and his own commitment to racial justice. When Nelson

Mandela made his historic visit to New York shortly after his release from prison, Browning was given the honor of introducing him at a major inter-church event.

There is no doubt that the end of apartheid during Browning's term was one of his most satisfying moments.

Acceptance Speech, General Convention, Anaheim, September 1985

I have this day sent a telex to Bishop Tutu offering the full support of my office to his courageous ministry. I have extended my sincere hope that he might be present for my installation next January 11th so that the occasion itself might sacramentally express our love and our support for this man and his people—an expression of our solidarity in the heart of the nation's capital.

Two years ago, I had the privilege of representing this Church as part of an international delegation appointed by the Archbishop of Canterbury to visit the war torn Diocese of Namibia. Namibia is a country held under the illegal administration of South Africa that applies the evil of apartheid to its peoples as well . . .

A Namibian Anglican layman, obviously the spokesman of the village (said to us), "Our sovereign is the Lord Jesus Christ—him and him alone do we serve. We want to witness to his love and share his life with all. We want to enjoy the freedoms you enjoy. We want our people to be freed of oppression—we want justice established—we want to stand equal with our white brothers and sisters—we want the war ended so life can be restored to the place of dignity—we want peace for our people in every respect—we want it because we know it is what God wills for us."

In looking at the brutality of apartheid, I am reminded of Thomas Jefferson's statement in addressing slavery, "I tremble for my country when I reflect that God is just."

Actions taken: Comments to Executive Council, June 17,1986

We meet as the situation in South Africa becomes more desperate. The world's attention is focused on the struggle between an oppressed black majority, seeking enfranchisement and the establishment of basic human rights, and the minority white government which seeks to preserve the institutional racist system of apartheid. For Episcopalians and our worldwide partners in the Anglican Communion our attention, our support and our hope are focused upon one brave, articulate and tireless man, Desmond Tutu. Tutu is both a fearless individual and the symbol of the Anglican Church's moral role in South Africa.

In this time of deepening crisis, I pledge my full support to Archbishop-elect Tutu and the forces of moderation and reconciliation he represents in South Africa. To this end, I would like to announce that I have taken the following actions;

1. I have sent a personal message of prayers and support to Archbishop Phillip Russell and to Archbishop-elect Tutu;

2. I have joined with the heads of other denominations in the United States in sending a letter to the President, Secretary of State and the congressional leadership asking for immediate diplomatic action to end apartheid in South Africa including strong economic sanctions;

3. I have joined in sending a message of support to the South African Council of Churches (SACC) and its General Secretary, the Rev. Byers Naude;

4. I have joined in sending a telegram to the Rev. Leon Sullivan requesting that he advance the date of his planned actions with United States corporations doing business in South Africa;

5. I have joined in personal letters to five United States banks, which continue to make loans to the government of South Africa, asking them to cancel all new loans and refuse to roll over existing loans as they come due;

6. I have joined in writing to twelve major United States corporations requesting them to review their current operations in South Africa, especially in providing materials and goods to the government and the South African Defense Forces.

To enable the Episcopal Church to achieve a firm grasp of the situation in South Africa, and the work of the Anglican Church there, I have concurred with the recommendation of the Education Staff, and have designated the 1986-1987 Church School Missionary Offering for the Archbishop Desmond Tutu South African Refugee Scholarship Fund.

I have asked the Presiding Bishop's Fund for World Relief, which has long worked through the Church in South Africa providing emergency relief, to continue and intensify its assistance. The fund will continue to provide education and leadership training, pastoral counselling, small business development and other forward looking programs which give hope to South Africa's youth. Such programs are vital to the future of a country, now divided by racism, if South Africans of all races are to fulfill their promise as leaders on the African continent. I ask all Episcopalians to join in this assistance by sending funds directly to the Presiding Bishop's Fund.

I welcome the initiative by the Archbishop of Canterbury in sending his special envoy, Mr. Terry Waite, to Johannesburg to provide us with a first-hand report on the situation. Mr. Waite leaves for South Africa today, and I think that he can be assured of all our prayers.

To express my personal support to Bishop Tutu and the Church of the Province of Southern Africa, I have informed Bishop Tutu that I will travel to South Africa to attend his enthronement as Archbishop of Cape Town on September 7th. The government of South Africa has been informed of this intention and I have made formal visa application.

It is my intention that our actions must be commensurate with our message. *The racist policy of apartheid must end.* I plan to use the persuasion of my office to proclaim this goal, and I will use the visibility of my office to support those who work peacefully for apartheid's demise.

Statement on implementing General Convention policy, June 11, 1987

A series of events in this country and in South Africa compel me to tell the Church, the US government and our sisters and brothers in South Africa: "We know we have more work to do, and we will do it."

Dr. Leon Sullivan, who led the first institutional efforts to break the apartheid stranglehold, now takes a further courageous step. The government of South Africa—buoyed by a shift to the right in recent all-white elections—now refuses to admit Dr. Sullivan after years of welcoming him to South Africa. Just at the end of May, Archbishop Desmond Tutu and other Soweto residents who have engaged in a rent strike against the government are threatened. It goes on and on and on.

The struggle for justice in Southern Africa commands the commitment of this Church toward all those who, at great personal risk, make no peace with oppression. Some of our actions are complete. Some are still underway and, in other cases, we need to make decisions about our role in South Africa's present turmoil and our role in her future.

Under mandate from General Convention, our Executive Council has divested all holdings in companies doing business with South Africa and Namibia. In addition, the Church Pension Fund, dioceses, parishes and affiliated institutions are now in various stages of disinvestment.

In 1985, the General Convention of the Episcopal Church also called on the United States government to develop "an unambiguous coherent policy in opposition to apartheid" that included the imposition of trade and other economic sanctions on the Republic of South Africa. While some of these sanctions have since become law, it is evident that no such coherent policy exists and that the clear voice of the Church is still needed.

Just as individuals have labored for peace and justice, so have some US corporations endeavored to improve the economic conditions of all South Africans. These are the ones who heard the calls of Dr. Sullivan, our own late, beloved Dr. Charles Lawrence and others and acted to improve the lot of their black workers and pressed for governmental reforms. Tragically, these steps have fallen short of ending apartheid. The time has come to call on the owners, managers and directors of these firms to continue to disinvest in their South African operations and facilities, or initiate such an orderly disinvestment process.

In calling on US companies to withdraw their investments from South Africa, we ask that this bold step be coupled with movement toward constructive change in the constitution and policies of South Africa. Any disinvestment which merely rearranges ownership while leaving intact policies or operations which support oppressive governmental acts cannot be judged as either ethically sound or economically pragmatic.

Conversely, any disinvestment which encourages sound black entrepreneurship is to be applauded, as are those methods which disengage companies from supplying goods and services to military and police establishments which are party to oppressive acts.

Our call for disinvestment is made with full recognition that such an action will impose special hardships upon black South Africans, and, in some cases, upon both US and South African employees of affected firms, as well as their owners. Nevertheless, Archbishop Tutu and other leaders of those who stand to be adversely affected by sanctions have steadily maintained that such economic pain is the price of justice. We who stand in solidarity with our brothers and sisters in South Africa recognize their sacrifice and ask their forgiveness for our past neglect which now contributes to their suffering. I pledge the continuing presence, actions and resources of the Episcopal Church to help relieve the suffering resulting from apartheid and to press for its end . . .

About Desmond Tutu: Sermon to the House of Bishops, San Antonio, September 1986

"The mass of men lead lives of quiet desperation," wrote Thoreau in *Walden*. But I believe that there are times when a man's desperation forbids *standing by in guilty silence*. When justice demands a loud voice, God raises up on an Amos or a Wilberforce. God has raised up a voice in our time. God has called Desmond Tutu to give voice and power to the desperation of his people in South Africa. I stand here today to give acclamation and support to his prophetic ministry.

In a recent newspaper interview, a young activist who admits being an admirer of Archbishop Tutu said: "The trouble with Desmond is that he is a prisoner of the Gospel. He says, 'love thine enemy.' At his age, he should hate a little bit more."

I have just returned from Cape Town and the enthronement of Desmond Tutu. Before I departed on the trip, I had received a number of letters demeaning the leadership of this man and decrying our solidarity with his Church's witness against the vile racist system of apartheid. Many expressed outrage at Tutu's comments following our President's recent address on South Africa. I have answered personally each of these letters, and I would like to share publicly with you my response. I wrote to each correspondent saying that living in the injustice of South Africa—in the suffering—in the midst of imprisonment and oppression—in almost a sea of hopelessness—with a minority government that refuses to have substantive political dialogue or recognize the dignity and worth of a majority of its people—living in these conditions, is it any wonder that this man of God would show impatience with the leaders of a nation that really could make the difference, that has a policy that is insensitive to the human realities, a policy which is called "constructive engagement," which is neither constructive nor engaging? Having been to South Africa, let me add a postscript. While in Cape Town, a beautiful city, a city which would rival any city in the Western world in cleanliness, I went with the Archbishop of Canterbury to the community called Crossroads, the squatter community which is being constantly harassed by the government. I stood in the ankle deep mud at the barbed wire which imprisons the blacks. I saw a squalor as I've never experienced before, and I have been around and seen a good deal. I witnessed the hovels which give shelter to mothers and children. No water, no sanitation, no education. Years of unemployment. No hope. No hope of employment. No hope at all. No future. One cannot, my friends, give that scene a pleasant face, there are no words adequate to describe the sense of desperation. As I stood there, I tasted the loss of humanity. There is no question in my mind that strong words are necessary and appropriate, even when addressed to world leaders, and that is where those words should be addressed.

The truth of the matter is that *Desmond Tutu* is a man of God—deeply spiritual, profoundly rooted in the biblical message of the Lord Incarnate. In my opinion, he will be remembered as a person not only of bravery and courage but one who personified the message of hope in a truly desperate situation. He is, indeed, a prisoner of the Gospel, and we can thank God that he is. Listen to his closing words of his enthronement sermon: "We shall be free, all of us, black and white, for it's God's intention. He enlists us to help Him to transfigure all the ugliness of this world into the beauty of His Kingdom. We shall be free, all of us, because the death and resurrection of Jesus Christ our Lord assures us that life has overcome death, light has overcome darkness, love has overcome hate, righteousness has overcome injustice and oppression, goodness has overcome evil, and that compassion and caring, laughter and joy, sharing and peace, reconciliation and forgiveness have overcome their awful counterparts in God's Kingdom, where God is all in all . . ."

The Tragedy of Apartheid: Address to Executive Council, Pittsburgh, June 13, 1989

I have now just returned with Patti from a two-week visit to the Church of the Province of Southern Africa. In Mozambique, we were shocked and deeply saddened at the savagery and cruelty of the violence. There is an appalling degree of sheer wantonness about this terrorism, aided and abetted by powers who want to see the frontline states [of Southern Africa] destabilized and weakened. On the other hand, the Church is alive and well in Mozambique, and we were privileged and humbled to be hosted by the courageous bishop of Lebombo, Dinis Sengulane . . .

One of the great tragedies of apartheid is that people are cut off from the richness of diversity and the gifts their neighbors have to offer. One afternoon in Durban we were taken through the various segregated townships surrounding that shining white city—areas set apart for Indians and Asians, for black Africans, for the so-called "Coloured." We met a family in one of those townships—Umlazi, it was—and talked for a long time together over tea in their living room. Our driver and guide was a white South African, a man committed to the struggle for equality. One of our group asked him if the white people in his own neighborhood ever visited the townships. He replied that probably 90 percent would spend their whole lives in Durban and never drive through such a township! Can you imagine what a tragedy this is? People with rich traditions of history, culture, ability, and insight living within a stone's throw of each other and yet so ignorant of the other's gifts. People of the most stimulating and enriching diversity almost shoulder to shoulder and yet unable to look into the other's eye and see there a member of the family . . .

On the release of Nelson Mandela, February 11, 1990

The release of Nelson Mandela is a welcome moment in the history of South Africa and hopefully a watershed moment in the struggle against apartheid. I extend to President de Klerk my gratitude for his leadership and good judgment in taking this action. And I share in the joy of millions of people in South Africa and around the globe that this day has finally come.

I extend to Nelson Mandela my personal greetings and the greetings of the Episcopal Church in the United States. We have prayed and worked with the anti-apartheid movement for many years to see this day arrive, a day that vindicates the right of all South Africans to have full participation in the country of their birth. This is a day for all those who have been a part of the long struggle against apartheid to rejoice and celebrate.

Now is not the time to ease economic pressures on South Africa. That must come when negotiations for a non-racial, democratic South Africa are clearly irreversible. As we celebrate this day, let us not be premature in thinking that apartheid is all but gone.

I urge all of us engaged in this struggle to be vigilant, and to provide the South African government with the incentives to move with haste to the dismantling of the system that the world abhors. It is a sad but truthful observation that power is rarely given up voluntarily.

Let us encourage President de Klerk to continue on this bold new course. We call now for an end to the state of emergency and the release of all political detainees. And we look to the Parliament to abolish all apartheid laws during its current session so that it can create a conducive climate for negotiations with Mr. Mandela and other legitimate black leadership.

Statement on the South African referendum, March 18, 1992

I am deeply relieved by the historic vote of the white community in South Africa calling for the end of apartheid by a significant margin. This vote is dramatic evidence of the desire of white South Africans to abandon the tragic and inhuman policies of apartheid . . .

While this vote is encouraging, I am dismayed by the violence that continues to plague South Africa. The daily atrocities are to be roundly condemned. This senselessness must stop. May violence give way to a spirit of reconciliation and the creation of a just society, and quickly.

The Episcopal Church in the United States is ready and eager to end its long campaign of economic sanctions and divestment. Such a step will be possible once the violence has ended and power has been transferred irreversibly to an interim government ensuring that white South Africa no longer can be in a position to thwart the will of the majority.

God bless Africa. Guide her leaders. Guard her children. And give her peace.

Ending the divestment campaign against South Africa, September 17, 1993

The time for which so many millions of people have waited and prayed and for which so many thousands have worked to see happen is finally here. The dismantling of apartheid has begun in earnest. A new South Africa is being born with a transition to a democratic, non-racist, non-discriminatory form of government.

Thanks be to God who gives us the victory through our Lord Jesus Christ!

As we celebrate this time of transition, I am thrilled to announce, following the September 10 action of the South African bishops and a statement from Archbishop Desmond Tutu, that our long campaign of economic pressure is over. As of this day the Episcopal Church ceases its divestment policy as established by the General Convention of 1985.

I have enormous admiration for our sisters and brothers in South Africa who have witnessed to the love of God in their long struggle against apartheid. And I want to commend those institutions of our own Church who supported our friends in South Africa by staying the course on divestment in the face of considerable opposition. No one today seriously doubts the effectiveness of the sanctions campaign . . .

So we move to a new phase in support of our partners in South Africa who prepare now for their first genuine democratic election. We were there for the long haul to see the end of one of history's great injustices. And now we will be there in the building of a new society based on democracy and nondiscrimination.

Address to Executive Council, Omaha, April 25, 1994

I think today of our partners in South Africa, where at this very moment history is being made. I rejoice that we have been a part of making that history . . .

I would ask now if we might join in silent prayer for all of the people of South Africa. Let us especially call to mind those men and women who will be free to vote for the very first time in the history of their land. Let us give thanks for the developments in South Africa, for the witness of the church, for the persons, living and dead, who have made their witness of hope, of justice. Amen.

AFRICA

The Presiding Bishop responded to a number of crises in Africa during his term, not always with a written statement, but often through staff visits and work with Anglican partners in the regions and generous support for humanitarian relief from the Presiding Bishop's Fund for World Relief for such places as Liberia and the Sudan.

Rwanda: Letter to President Clinton, May 3, 1994

I am alarmed to learn that 500 Rwandans being held hostage in the Mille Collines hotel, Kigali, are threatened with execution this Friday unless military officers are released by the Rwandan Patriotic Front. I urge an all-out diplomatic effort by the United Nations to seek the immediate release and safe passage of these hostages.

I believe your intervention is needed to procure the release of these people, who, I'm told, are out of food and are drinking water from the hotel swimming pool.

I deeply appreciate your leadership in summoning the international community to take steps to restore order in Rwanda and pray for quick and effective action in ending the horrors that have consumed the country.

May I ask, in addition to this urgent request, that you consider seriously, through the office of the Attorney General, granting temporary protective status to Rwandans in the United States whose visas may be about to expire. This would be in the best tradition of our country's concern for displaced persons in a time of tyranny and chaos.

God bless you for your efforts.

Letter to George Carey, Archbishop of Canterbury, October 31, 1994

I have been hearing a number of accounts of events related

to our Church's role in Rwanda. I was disturbed by a news article in a Ugandan paper while I was there recently which implicated Church leadership in the recent crisis.

My understanding is that all but one of our bishops have left Rwanda, most of them to Nairobi. I gather most of the priests and laity are either in the country or in refugee camps. The separation of the bishops from their priests and lay members alarms me. I see the potential for deep divisions within the Church that may prove very difficult to heal. I am certainly not judging the decision of the bishops to leave, only noting possible consequences the longer they stay away. The Roman Catholic bishops made a decision to remain in the country and three of them have paid with their lives . . .

Uganda and AIDS: Address to Executive Council, New York City, November 1, 1994

The week that we spent in Uganda in early October was full of faces and experiences that we will not soon forget. About nine years ago, after two decades of terrorism and civil war, the nation began to recover slowly under a stable presidency.

To give you some idea of what the problems are, I can say that, out of a population of approximately 17 million persons in a state the size of Oregon, 400,000 are orphans. These children were left alone as a result of the years of war, and of AIDS, which is ravaging the country. Eighty percent of Ugandans are Christians, and about half of those are Anglicans so the role of the church has been pivotal in rebuilding the nation. The Church of Uganda has made a valiant witness. We can be proud to be their partners.

At one of our stops, a young priest spoke to me, took my hand, and said: "When you go home, please tell your church, please tell them, knowing that you care about us means everything to us. It just means everything to us." How could I fail to deliver that message?

THE MIDDLE EAST
Search for a lasting peace

The Presiding Bishop broke new ground on the intractable problem of Israel and Palestine during his term of office, bringing about a transformation of church policy in support of the rights of Palestinians. It seems peculiar that with a partner church made up of Palestinians the Episcopal Church had been so slow to recognize their grievances against the state of Israel. But the aftermath of the holocaust seemed to rivet the Episcopal Church's attention on the plight of Jews while largely ignoring Anglican Palestinians. Criticism of the state of Israel has often been interpreted as anti-semitism, especially among sensitive Jewish leaders.

Browning, however, pursued an even handed approach and chose to defend both the aspirations of Palestinians and Israel's right to exist. This was consistent with the long time position of the World Council of Churches. Despite his support for Israel's security, Browning, like the WCC, was criticized many times by Jewish leader for befriending Yasser Arafat and advocating a Palestinian state.

He was also criticized by members of his own church. But Browning refused to budge, claiming that support for a just peace in the region, including security for Israel, could not be construed as anti-semitism.

On two occasions before the Oslo accord in 1994, Browning met Yasser Arafat in Geneva and Tunis to assure him that not all Americans opposed the rights of Palestinians and encouraged him to pursue negotiations with the Israelis.

Small support groups for Palestinians began to form in the Episcopal Church and eventually major policies were established at General Convention which for the first time were critical of Israel. These included calling for withholding of US aid to Israel and challenging Israel's unilateral claim to Jerusalem. Groups of Episcopalians such as the church's Commission on Peace traveled to the region and were hosted by the Anglican Church instead of the Israeli tourist authority.

Browning's leadership helped the church to focus on some blind spots in America's view of Israel, particularly its brutal occupation of the West Bank and Gaza and many charges of human rights abuses.

As time wore on, two issues threatened any eventual peace between Israel and the Palestinians—first, the claim of Israel to all of Jerusalem as its capital; second, the development of Jewish settlements in the West Bank and Gaza, especially in and around East Jerusalem.

The fact that an agreement was reached and a peace process begun, which included the return of Yasser Arafat to Gaza and the West Bank, and that some control of the territories was turned over to the Palestinians, was a remarkable accomplishment. Browning was among those in attendance at the White House when Rabin and Arafat shook hands September 13, 1994.

No account of Browning's witness in the Israeli/Palestinian issue can exclude mention of the contributions of his wife, Patti. She brought enormous energy and passion to the issue in her own right. Mrs. Browning made annual visits to the area and helped raise the consciousness of thousands of Episcopalians through her many activities.

Browning began to express his Middle East concerns with a statement on Libyan terrorism which remains as poignant as when he first made it:

Statement on terrorism and US attack on Libya, April 1980

The US military action against the Republic of Libya is a serious unilateral action with grave consequences.

Terrorism is a growing cancer within the body of our global community. It is a reaction on the part of those convinced that without violent measures, their grievances will not be addressed. Clearly, no responsible government can make peace with terrorism, terrorists, or those who support them. At the same time, it is the height of irresponsibility not to address the underlying causes, thereby showing moderate elements in the Middle East that avenues to the resolution of long-standing grievances other than terrorism exist. By making terrorism unnecessary, we cut terrorists off from their support bases as well as their reason for being.

Although one can and does abhor terrorism and seeks its eradication, the quality of the response must witness to the maturity of the policy and decision-making process. Before using force, has every alternative avenue of response been explored? Is the response proportionate? Is the action to be effective rather than efficient and expeditious? Does the action produce international trust and cooperation?

In the days ahead, I hope that we will reflect on the long term consequences of our actions and not on the seeming immediate sense of gratification. I pray that the motivations and course of our actions will be consistent with the purity of our intentions and that they truly reflect our search for a lasting peace in the Middle East. To that end, I respectfully ask that the President withdraw our forces and make it clear to the world that this has been a measured effort to bring the blight of terrorism to an end.

Reflections in a letter to *The Episcopalian*, March 1987

[I visited]:

*A Syrian prelate in Jerusalem who delighted and warmed our group and a group of Israeli officials who were visiting at the same time by singing "We Shall Overcome" in Aramaic—

quickly reminding us that this was the language of the Lord.

*A young Arab man and a tiny dynamo of a Palestinian woman, directors of the YMCA and YWCA in East Jerusalem, who strive with energy from every part of their being to give young men and women the sense of dignity that will break the yoke of generations of hate which has been generated out of decades of living in refugee camps.

Easter message, 1988

Over the past months we have seen and read about the violent confrontations in the occupied territories of Gaza and the West Bank. It is a tragic situation which goes beyond inter-religious tensions. Over one hundred people have been killed. Schools have been closed for over four months. Homes and farms have been destroyed in acts of rage. Day by day the tension and frustration mounts.

We cannot, however, allow ourselves to become judges of this situation. Rather, we have to ask ourselves: What constructive role can the Christian community, notably the Episcopal Church, play in resolving this situation in a land which is a part of our heritage as well?

In an effort to explore this, I sent a team to the Middle East to examine the situation there and to report back to me. This they have now done. I want to share with you at this early date some immediate responses, knowing that many details need to be worked out and that long-range planning still needs to be done. But, the suffering is now and we must respond.

Following upon their report I have decided upon the following course of action for the Episcopal Church:

1. I have asked for a greater support of the Good Friday Offering. I urge every parish and diocese, if they have not already done so, to send this offering to the Church Center immediately.

2.   I am launching a Special Appeal, through the Presiding Bishop's Fund for World Relief, for the Diocese of Jerusalem.
3.   I have asked the staff at the Church Center to develop educational resources regarding the Middle East so that parishes may study this situation during the Easter season.
4.   I am forming a committee of distinguished Episcopalians to advise me on issues in the region and appropriate, constructive responses to the complexities that prevent justice, peace and security for all people in the land we call "holy".

Letter to President Bush, September 10, 1991

I greatly welcome your leadership in advancing the peace process in the Middle East. While we had our differences over the Gulf crisis a few months ago, I could not be more supportive of your efforts to generate a peace conference in the Middle East.

Your willingness to name Israeli settlements in the occupied territories as a continuing barrier to peace is both courageous and proper. I believe such a position can only improve Arab trust of US good intentions to achieve a just peace.

Specifically, I am very pleased to read of your position to delay guarantees of $10 billion in housing loans until the peace process has at least begun. I am prepared to support this effort in any way that might be helpful. May I add that the role of Jim Baker has been absolutely superb. We are all blessed by his initiative for this conference. I hold the both of you in my prayers.

Thank you, dear sir, for the impartial way you are seeking a just peace for all of the Middle East. We are a much stronger nation when we seek justice rather than advantage.

Letter to Assistant Secretaries of State Edward P. Djerejian and Patricia Diaz, October 13, 1992

I write to ask in what ways your office is responding to the current situation in Israeli prisons. The decision by Israel to investigate Palestinian prisoner complaints and the subsequent suspension of the prisoners' hunger strike is a positive development. However, those of us who have traveled extensively to this area and are regularly informed by our friends in Israel/Palestine know that human rights abuses are real, brutal daily occurrences and a clear violation of international standards.

I particularly would like to know what steps your office is taking to protect Mr. Ahmad Qatamesh (ID #98370264) who is reportedly under hooded interrogation, sleep deprivation and other physical abuses. I have heard enough first hand reports of this kind of torture to raise my level of concern in this case.

The US government, as the major benefactor of the Israeli government, has a crucial obligation to assure itself that such funding is not involved in perpetuating human rights abuses. I wish to be assured by you that our government is using all diplomatic means at its disposal to call the Israeli government to account for its treatment of Palestinian prisoners.

Letter to James Baker, Secretary of State, August 13, 1992

I want to advise you that I have accepted an invitation to meet next week in Tunis to consult with the Palestinian National Council. While I am not certain what may be on Mr. Arafat's agenda, I will take my own message of support for the peace process. This meeting has been facilitated by some Church leaders in the Middle East.

I am anxious to better understand the agreement on the housing loan guarantees prior to my departure and am seeking help on this through our partner Church in Jerusalem.

You are never far from my thoughts and prayers in these critical days.

Letter to a fellow bishop, March 22, 1993

Here's my position and this Church's. I support peace and security for Israel and sovereignty for the Palestinians. Is this not a reasonable position? What I deplore is the incredible distortion in this country which makes everything Arab evil and everything Israeli good. This distortion, lived out in funneling billions of dollars to Israel without accountability, staggers me. When it comes to Israel, otherwise good and just people throw truth to the wind and pretend the atrocities of Israeli occupation don't occur.

I can commend your support for the state of Israel. I share it. But I cannot condone your contention that because Israel elects its government, it doesn't commit serious human rights abuses. The abuses are documented and the accounts are brutal.

There is no doubt in my mind that the abuses of Israeli occupation have fed the rise of the HAMAS and undermined moderate voices. I only wish that an international peacekeeping force could replace the presence of the Israeli army in the occupied territories.

We will long disagree on this matter, and that seems certain. And it pains me too. You remain for me a dear friend, and I am glad we can speak openly to one another.

Statement on the Israeli-Palestinian peace accord, September 13, 1993

This is the day the Lord has made. Let us rejoice and be glad in it.

The joy I felt in seeing the historic signing of peace between Israel and the Palestinians goes beyond words. My whole being was lifted up and my hope for the future is renewed.

That was such a great moment. The people from the land that gave birth to the three great religions of Islam, Judaism and Christianity have decided they can make peace. They have decided they can live together. That is a moment to celebrate.

This pact for peace, while only a first step, and yet a gigantic one, is a resounding affirmation of the highest values that the three great religions of the region share in common. It is as it should be. The values of love, hope, peace and justice now have a chance to triumph over hatred, suspicion, racism and violence.

Arabs and Jews, and Muslims and Christians from the Middle East who take this bold step today, serve as an inspiration to the whole human race. Let those engaged in acts of violence everywhere take note. Let those who fight and commit atrocities because of differences over religion, ethnicity or ideology be chastened by the nobleness of spirit we see emerging from the cradle of our three faith groups.

I extend my utmost congratulations to all those who have served the cause of peace and brought about this new day, especially to Prime Minister Rabin and Chairman Arafat. May we all join hands together in celebration and continue the journey to be one human family, reconciled and made whole.

Statement on the Hebron massacre, March 3, 1994

I join with Jewish, Muslim and Christian voices everywhere who condemn the Hebron massacre. I grieve with the families of the victims and am outraged at the fanatical elements that caused it.

The massacre lays bare one of the great obstacles to peace in Israel/Palestine, namely the issue of settlements. While I condemn extremism and violence on all sides, Israel cannot justify a policy that arms settlers, creating a paramilitary force in the territories. Israel's decision to disarm the settlers must be total, not selective, and anything short of complete disarmament is unacceptable. The Israeli government policy of allowing settlers to be armed while denying Palestinians the same right of self-protection from Israeli extremists is simply wrong.

Further, I call for the future status of the settlements to be resolved now. Israel's policy on settlements, including ongoing work on existing settlements (especially in and around East Jerusalem), is a serious drawback to the issue of sovereignty for a future Palestinian State. The integrity of a two-state solution demands resolution of this contentious issue in the context of current negotiations. Until this matter is resolved, I call for the suspension of any further loan guarantees to Israel.

I have long advocated for international protection of Palestinians in the territories. The Hebron massacre redoubles my conviction and I call for the United Nations to make such protection available at once. I plead with my own government to end its unjust opposition at the United Nations to such protection.

The truth is that Israel has a shameful human rights record through its years of occupation. I know it, my government knows it, the world knows it and it is a disgrace to deny the offer of international protection for one more day. The United States stands for human rights as a linchpin of its foreign policy. It is time to implement that policy in the Israeli/Palestinian conflict.

Finally, it is my prayer this day that out of the terrible tragedy in Hebron can emerge the transformation needed to break the present impasse with a determination on all sides to sit together and produce the just and lasting peace the people of the region so desperately deserve.

Easter statement by Browning and Samir Kafity, President Bishop of Jerusalem and the Middle East, April 4, 1994

Christ is risen. Alleluia! "Peace I leave with you. My peace I give you."

For these last ten days we have been on a pilgrimage in the

Holy Land; a spiritual journey consecrated to the cause of peace for the peoples of this region. Along with our companions we traveled to the land of Egypt, where God called his people forth into a covenant with him; and to Damascus and the place where Paul's vision was restored after his conversion. In Damascus we met with one of our ecumenical partners from Iraq who told us of the suffering of millions of innocent people in the aftermath of the Gulf war and the ensuing sanctions. We came away convinced that the international community needs to end these sanctions and provide humanitarian relief and work for peace with the same energy with which it prepared for war.

We continued to Amman in the land that Jesus walked, and to Jerusalem, the site of God's mightiest act in the death and resurrection of Jesus. Here we celebrated the rites of Maundy Thursday, Good Friday and Easter. We also visited the Gaza and passed through Hebron, the site of the recent massacre.

We said our prayers and we listened to the voices of the people. We listened to Christians from the Orthodox and Latin traditions speak of the difficulty of being a Christian in the Middle East when so-called "Christian countries in the West demonize all Arabs and Muslims as terrorists." And we broke bread with the Grand Mufti of Syria of the Muslim faith. We accepted his challenge to work for peace across Christian/Muslim boundaries as a prelude to a tripartite dialogue.

We were graciously received by the President of Egypt, the King of Jordan and the Prime Minister of Israel. And we found enormous good will among them for the cause of peace.

Most of all we listened to and prayed with those who suffer from persecution, hate, fear and oppression. By their witness and courage we have been spiritually renewed for our own ministries.

Our pilgrimage experience has strengthened our resolve to continue our witness for peace in this land. We reaffirm our partnership and solidarity with one another as leaders of our respective regional churches. We invite other Provinces of the

Anglican Communion to join with us in this unique partnership.

We reaffirm our commitment to support the creation of a sovereign state for a new Palestine while assuring peace and security for Israel.

We express our dismay at the uneven approach to the Israeli/Palestinian problem by the United States government for so many years and deplore the uncritical support of many members of the US Congress for positions of the Israeli lobby in Washington. Palestinians may not have equal access to the halls of Congress, but they are no less deserving of justice.

We note with equal dismay President Bill Clinton's repeated campaign position that Jerusalem be the capital of Israel. We consider this to be an unfortunate capitulation to the Israeli lobby. Although claiming to express his personal view, the President put that opinion into policy as a result of the US abstention on the United Nations resolution vote which referred to East Jerusalem as occupied territory. In adopting this disturbing position, President Clinton overlooks the profound issue of Jerusalem as a city sacred to Muslims and Christians as well as Jews. We oppose any agreement that would allow one faith to monopolize control of the holy places. Genuine peace for the holy city of Jerusalem must respect, equally, all three Abrahamic faiths.

We were appalled at the misery of Palestinians living in Gaza without the most basic of human services and the complete absence of fundamental human rights. Washington can best serve the cause of peace by assuring the strong economic development of a Palestine free from occupation and oppression. We believe this can be best demonstrated by generosity to a sovereign Palestine commensurate with its generosity to Israel, assuring the peace and prosperity of both Israel and the new Palestine.

Despite assurances to the United States government by Israel, we saw the construction of settlements continuing at an alarming rate. This exasperating policy by Israel remains a deep impediment to the peace process. A Palestinian voice aptly referred to the settlements as a cancer in the peace process. We urgently seek an end to US loan guarantees and the withholding of aid until this practice has ceased once and for all.

While not having time to visit Nazareth and Galilee, Palestinians from the area came to us and pleaded that the rights of Arabs living in Israel not be lost in the peace process. We note with deep concern the contention of Arabs in Israel that democracy excludes them.

We believe that true peace for both Palestinians and Israelis and all the peoples of the Middle East must be built on the goodwill of men and women on all sides in all places. The deepest values of the three Abrahamic faiths call us into a relationship with one another based on justice and mutual respect.

Statement on Afula killings, April 8, 1994

I condemn completely, the fanatical attack on innocent people at a bus stop in Afula, Israel. And I am deeply saddened at the pain of the families who lost relatives in this senseless act. Revenge serves no good purpose.

Prime Minister Rabin said to me in a meeting March 31 that the best response to violence is to implement the Declaration of Principles as quickly as possible. I heartily agree.

The sooner the occupation of the West Bank and Gaza ends, the sooner Palestinians can move towards sovereignty and Israel towards peace and security. The course of violence cannot be allowed to succeed. The peace process cannot be allowed to fail.

Address to Executive Council in Omaha, April 25, 1994

Our recent visit to the Middle East, on behalf of us all, is a symbol of our commitment to our partnership. If only I could share with you what the support and prayers of this church mean to the tiny struggling church in Egypt. If only you could spend an hour with me in the Diocese of Jerusalem, where, under conditions that make you want to throw up your hands in despair, faithful Christians follow in the steps of Jesus—loving and healing on a daily, hourly basis—in the very land where he walked. Our love, our caring means everything in the world to our partners in the Middle East, just as their witness, in the face of almost indescribable adversity, means everything to us. That kind of witness brings fresh springs to nurture our faith. We must never abandon one another, anymore than God will abandon us.

Statement on Jordanian/Israeli agreement, November 1, 1994

I want to express my congratulations to King Hussein and Prime Minister Rabin and all the people of Israel and Jordan on their historic peace agreement. The resolution of the essential issue of territorial claims is crucial to the long term cause of peace in the region.

I also want to take this moment to condemn in the strongest terms those who thwart the peace process through heinous acts of violence. Recent terrorist acts against innocent Israelis are revolting and cowardly tactics that deserve the thorough scorn of the international community. I weep for the families of those who lost their loved ones in these atrocities. Such acts of hate and vengeance show us all how fragile the peace process is.

While peace is moving forward in the region despite many snares, I am moved to remind all parties that the most difficult issue of all lies ahead, that being the final status of Jerusalem. Israel's continuing construction and expansion of settlements in and around occupied East Jerusalem remains a blatant attempt to create "facts on the ground" in violation of international law. Since the signing of the Declaration of Principles in September, 1993, settlements have expanded by an estimated 33 percent. I cannot stress enough how seriously this continuing activity impedes the hope for a just peace.

Letter to Anthony Lake, National Security Advisor, June 29, 1995

I express my concern over the Congressional effort to move the US embassy from Tel Aviv to Jerusalem. I want to underscore my support for the administration's policy to oppose such a move. I need not rehearse with you the complications such a move would cause for the peace process. Our government relations office has actively communicated the Church's position to Congress and we want to coordinate our efforts with the Administration on this crucial issue.

Statement on the assassination of Yitzhak Rabin, November 6, 1995

Like so many people all over the world, I am deeply shaken over the assassination of Yitzhak Rabin. The world has lost a courageous peacemaker, a man who lived as a soldier and fought and plotted against an enemy of over forty years. But his true moment of glory and hardest battle began when he took up the cause of peace and uttered those profound words two years ago by reminding us you don't make peace with your friends. You make peace with your enemies.

I was so elated to be present when he transformed those words into a spectacular reality as he shook hands with his old enemy, Chairman Yasser Arafat of the PLO, on the White House lawn in September 1993.

During the pilgrimage to the Middle East in 1994, I met the Prime Minister in Tel Aviv shortly after the Hebron massacre, and we shared our deep sorrow over that tragedy. And he stressed in that strong and articulate voice of his that no act of terrorism or violence could be allowed to derail the peace process. Now he is a victim of violence and a martyr for peace and his words become a challenge for those left behind to continue in his work.

Statement to the Christian Conference on Jerusalem, January 23, 1996

I greet you all in the name of the one God of Abraham, who I believe calls all peoples of this region into full peace with one another.

I commend the planners of this conference for convening this gathering. The importance of Jerusalem to Christians around the world cannot be overstated. While Jesus was born in Bethlehem, it was his death and Resurrection in Jerusalem that gave birth to our faith. When Christians look at their roots and seek to understand their faith, they look to Jerusalem. Jerusalem and Christianity are inseparable. Your gathering here underscores this vital relationship between the faith of Christianity and this holy and revered city.

As Christians make their rightful claim to this place, we also recognize that Muslims and Jews have equal and powerful claims to Jerusalem from their perspectives. It is pointless and futile for any one of the three religions to argue a greater claim to the city than another. Instead, we need a spirit of mutual respect among us to guide the future of Jerusalem.

Today, the government of Israel and the emerging state of Palestine have made immense and courageous steps toward peace. I salute both parties for their resolute determination to find a way to live together in peace and security. This is a noble undertaking.

We know as well that the hardest part of the negotiations lie ahead as the future of this city is still to be decided. I am compelled to say that as these negotiations move forward, no number of Israeli settlements, no number of detentions, no number of confiscations, no votes of the US Congress can change what we all know: the sovereignty of Jerusalem is claimed equally by Palestinians as it is by Israel. And no unilateral action by one side can be accepted as valid by the international community. Only mutual agreement can shape the future of city.

The task of the three Abrahamic faiths is to bring together the best of our traditions to influence a future Jerusalem. We must bring our values for justice, mutual respect, and love to the peace process. Our voices, led by Palestinians and Jews of the three faiths, hold the best chance for achieving genuine reconciliation and harmony.

Statement on the outbreak of violence between Israelis and Palestinians, September 27, 1996

I implore the government of Israel and the Palestinian Authority (PA) to work together to end the tragic outbreak of violence in the Gaza and West Bank, including East Jerusalem. I advocate an immediate return to the peace process. This is a time when both sides must demonstrate their resolve to end the current stalemate.

My fear is that unless there is dramatic movement on a swift return to the peace process, the leadership of the two sides could lose control of events. Already, more will be required than another handshake. The peace process has to move from posturing to substance. Despite Prime Minister Netanyahu's encouraging meeting with PA President Yasser Arafat and an assurance of a commitment to the peace process, no progress is visible.

Recent actions by Israel have inflamed passions not seen since the *intifada*. Among those actions are the ending of a four-year freeze on construction in Jewish settlements in the West Bank, a demand to shut down Palestinian offices in Jerusalem and continued refusal to withdraw from Hebron. Confiscations and demolitions of Arab land in and around Jerusalem also continue, including inside the Old City. The most recent action is the opening of a new gate in a long-disputed tunnel next to the Arab Quarter of the Old City which precipitated the present outbreak of violence.

Negotiations for the future of Jerusalem must begin in earnest. There will be no peace and no justice unless the aspirations of Jews, Muslims and Christians are respected in final negotiations. Unilateral claims to Jerusalem are unacceptable and are a prescription for a long and tragic conflict.

I call upon the United States as the principal sponsor of the peace talks to assure both parties that the future of Jerusalem must be negotiated between the two sides. I also encourage Israel to end its tactics of creating "facts on the ground." As a first step, I appeal to the Israeli government to abandon its ill-advised decision to open a new gate into the Old City.

Finally, I join in expressing my grief for all those who have died or been wounded in the current violence. My prayers are with them and their families. The victims are on both sides. Only a resolve by the two parties to reach a just peace founded on good-faith negotiations will bring any redemption out of this latest tragedy.

Gulf War

Nothing inflamed Bishop Browning's passion more than the rush to war after the invasion of Kuwait. He would later say that the war and the Los Angeles riots were his saddest moments as Presiding Bishop.

Browning was seen by ecumenical partners as the leader who brought the religious community together in opposition to the war. He began by assembling selected staff to focus on the crisis shortly after the invasion in August, 1990, and then he convened, through a series of conference calls, meetings of religious leaders. They issued joint statements and eventually traveled to the Middle East, with Browning going to Baghdad.

They asked for a meeting with George Bush, who agreed to see only Browning. He flew via the Concorde from Paris in a mad scramble home from Baghdad to make that

appointment. He met with Bush and Secretary of State James Baker alone in the oval office. Bush showed Browning an Amnesty International report critical of Saddam Hussein's human rights record in Kuwait. Browning countered that he would welcome seeing the administration's support for human rights in other parts of the Middle East, including the Occupied Territories. In the end, the two sides agreed to disagree about the impending war.

On the night before the war started, January 15, 1991, Browning led a march from the Washington Cathedral to the White House and observed an all-night vigil in a nearby church praying that war might be averted. The next morning he called the President and offered to go over and pray with him. Bush declined the offer, but spoke with him and accepted his prayers. Later media reports said Browning had refused to see the President who called on Billy Graham instead. It was true that Graham was a guest of the President during that time, but Browning had most assuredly asked to be with the President. The following day James Baker called Browning and asked him to lead him in prayer.

Early on, Browning had supported Bush's sanctions policy as a way to induce Saddam Hussein to abandon Kuwait. But after the war, as sanctions continued, Browning was told by church leaders in Iraq, and by King Hussein of Jordan, that the sanctions were causing untold suffering. A suppressed report from a UN agency estimated half a million children were dying or would soon die from the sanctions. Browning, haunted by the face of a child he had seen in Baghdad, decided the suffering must end and called on now President Clinton to end the sanctions campaign. A proposal to exchange oil for humanitarian aid was refused by Saddam as a breach of sovereignty.

On July 12, 1995, Bishop Browning met with Nazir

Hamdoon, permanent representative of Iraq to the United Nations, to discuss the sanctions issue and also to plead for the release of two American prisoners in Iraq who had been captured along the Iraqi border. The Presiding Bishop expressed his interest in pursuing the sale of Iraqi oil through a third party to preserve Iraqi sovereignty, then using the profit for humanitarian needs. Hamdoon insisted Iraq was complying with UN resolutions and that all sanctions should be ended. He also said that the US prisoners would be released in a few days. They were, but sanctions continued unabated as US and Iraqi interpretation of UN resolutions differed.

Statement on the Persian Gulf crisis, October 5, 1990

I reach out to all people of goodwill during this time of international crisis in the Middle East. For these past weeks I have felt the pain and anguish that this crisis has wrought. My heart has been with the young men and women of the armed forces serving in Saudi Arabia, and with all those who find themselves displaced and refugees. My heart has been with all those persons in the Middle East who would be victims in the outbreak of war. And my heart has been with those who cry out for a peaceful resolution to this crisis.

With all these things and so much more weighing on my heart, I share my own thoughts as they have developed in these recent days. I offer them in a spirit of hope that in responding to this crisis with reason and compassion, we may find a peaceful resolve.

I believe that the United Nations' sanctions against Iraq are just and sound. The international community has come together in an unprecedented way to resist the naked aggression of one state against another. Iraq must now heed the judgment of the community of nations—including other Arab states—and withdraw completely from Kuwait while an embracing diplomatic solution is sought for the complex, interlocking problems of the Middle East as a whole.

But in spite of the near unanimity of the United Nations in confronting the crisis, the time is fraught with danger. Lines have been drawn in the desert sands. Huge armies and armadas, led by those of our own country, face each other with the promise of unimaginable destruction and havoc. Ironically, all this occurs just as the superpowers have moved from postures of confrontation to cooperation, and as the promise of a "peace dividend" has raised hopes in our country of a renewed emphasis on pressing national problems.

In this atmosphere of tension and the threat of war, let me, as Presiding Bishop of the Episcopal Church, urge the following of our people: That we not demonize, stereotype, or oversimplify.

This is not a time for propaganda but for sober truth. As the President Bishop of the Episcopal Church in Jerusalem and the Middle East has reminded us, the present conflict has a history and cannot be seen or dealt with in isolation. Part of that history is the arbitrary and self-serving manipulations of the colonial powers 70 years ago, manipulations that still engender rage among the Arab peoples and make all Western talk of democracy and justice sound to them like sheer hypocrisy.

The Persian Gulf crisis is made more complex and nearly intractable by the Palestinian problem, which lies at the core of Middle East unrest. But there is hope here, for if the present crisis can be resolved through United Nations sanctions and diplomatic means, the way may be paved for a long sought solution to the Palestinian problem. This is all the more reason that the crisis be seen in its true light as one part of an interconnected whole and not as an isolated incident.

Nor is the crisis a clash between Islam and Christianity, as the Archbishop of Canterbury so clearly stated in a recent speech to the British House of Lords. (Indeed, there is a sizable indigenous Christian community in Iraq, and the Anglican Diocese of Cyprus and the Gulf is present throughout the area.) Nor should we allow the crisis to degenerate into an anti-Arab campaign. Here the problem of stereotyping and demonization becomes acute. Americans must realize that the Saddam Hussein characterized as an Adolf Hitler after his invasion of Kuwait is the same person who a few weeks earlier was being touted by the Bush administration as a possible guarantor of peace and stability in the region. Surely truth and justice are not served by stereotype and propagandistic demonization.

Let me urge that we not fall into the trap of war as a means of solving the problem. The General Convention has endorsed numerous Lambeth Conference resolutions that "war as a method of settling international disputes is incompatible with the teaching and example of Our Lord Jesus Christ." Although the cold war is palpably dead, old cold war habits die hard. Does not the movement of a massive war machine to the deserts of Saudi Arabia and the waters of the Persian Gulf make war the more likely? The sanctions must be given time to work. I continue to believe firmly that the United Nations and the Arab states themselves, working in concert, offer the best hope for a bloodless solution to the conflict.

Let me urge that our national motives be clear and honorable. For what reason has our nation unleashed the greatest military force since the Vietnam War? Are we not justified in suspecting that the reason is primarily economic, having to do with unimpeded access to oil? Have we not sent our young men and women to the Persian Gulf, as our President has said, to "protect the American way of life"? But what way of life is it that allows the homeless and unemployed to huddle on our streets and our inner cities to decay? Is it possible that the American "way of life"—unbridled consumption—has become for many millions a "way of death," unendurable poverty? Let us examine our national priorities and our addiction to unnecessary consumption. Let us be the nation we imagine ourselves to be—a beacon to the world's poor, a standard-bearer for justice and peace.

Let me urge, finally, that we honor human life. With the brutal Iraqi invasion, innocent human beings have become pawns, shields, and hostages. Families have been separated. National economies in Jordan, Pakistan, Sri Lanka, the Philippines, and elsewhere have been strained by the sudden influx of refugees who have lost their possessions and their livelihoods. American women and men in the armed forces are serving bravely in a hostile and unknown environment, while their families tremble at home. As someone has said, "Old men and women should not be sending young men and women to die for mistakes made by those same old men and women." Misplaced priorities and mistaken decisions always exact a human cost. Shall this cost be the deaths of innocent civilians and brave young soldiers?

I pray for President Bush that he adhere to the United Nations resolutions on the Persian Gulf crisis, and I pray for him as he wrestles with the difficult decisions of his office. I urge that he remain steadfast and never give in to the trap of war.

I urge you, my fellow Episcopalians, to offer the same prayers. Join me in supporting cooperative and peaceful solutions to the crisis. Re-examine in a spirit of humble repentance your stewardship of the earth's resources. Resist the misplaced national pride that refuses to recognize the face of Christ in your brother and sister in Iraq and the Middle East. Love the Lord God with all your heart, and your neighbor as yourself. Pray for the peace of Jerusalem, and of all God's holy creation.

Message to Episcopalians, January 17, 1991

What we have feared has come to pass. What lies ahead only God knows. We hold in our hearts all who are caught in the agony of battle. Particularly we pray for the brave men and women of the military forces, for those who wait at home, and for all the innocent caught in the horror of the battle.

The future is unclear but our response is certain, and we turn to God in prayer.

Let us pray:
that the conflict may come to a speedy and decisive end, and that those at risk be safely delivered;
that the relationships of the nations be healed;
that weapons of mass destruction not be used;
that our spirits are not inflamed by hatred;
that international humanitarian law (the "Geneva Conventions") be strictly applied and adhered to;
that refugees find safe haven in countries removed from the conflict;
that we may be granted the spirit of repentance and reconciliation;
that our President, George, be upheld by our prayers, and that he and all the leaders of the nations may be guided in their decisions by the Spirit of mercy and peace.

I have directed the Presiding Bishop's Fund for World Relief and Episcopal Migration Ministry to join worldwide ecumenical efforts seeking to provide humanitarian aid to displaced persons and other victims, without distinction. The fund is acting in concert with the Office of the Suffragan Bishop for the Armed Forces to provide material aid and pastoral care to the dependents of our men and women serving in the war zone. I urge you to give generously to those whose needs are now so great. I must emphasize here that many thousands of faithful people in this country and abroad have prayed and marched for a peaceful resolution of the [Persian] Gulf crisis. Some, myself included, have long believed that war was uncalled for, that options short of war were far from being exhausted. It is now left for us to continue to pray and work for peace. I am heartened that people around our church are doing just that. Even in the heat of battle let us not forget that the call to peacemaking is an imperative for Christians. I will continue my peacemaking efforts in cooperation with other religious leaders. Strategies for peacemaking will develop as events unfold, and I will share them with you. Such efforts must continue in strength, and be guided by repentance rather than righteousness. My dear friends, in closing I want to tell you that I know we are fearful. Let us acknowledge our fears before God and ask that we may feel the sheltering arms of Jesus Christ. Our fear, our anguish, our grief is part of our humanity. We could not be alive to our world's realities and remain untouched by its pain, nor would we want to be untouched. As we follow in the path of Christ, we mold ours into compassionate hearts, and we open ourselves, as he did, to the wounds that come from loving. Let us make ourselves vulnerable in this way, knowing that Christ will take our pain and transform us. May the peace of God that passes all understanding be with all of his global family.

Remarks to US delegates at VII Assembly of the World Council of Churches, Canberra, Australia, February 8, 1991

Only a year ago, as preparations for this Seventh Assembly began to move into high gear, who among us would have predicted that our nation would today be at war in the Middle East? We had every reason then to look forward with confidence to a new world order. The Berlin Wall had fallen. The Cold War was over. Nelson Mandela was free.

But our confidence and optimism have been severely shaken since August 2nd. A great shadow has fallen over what appeared to be a bright new landscape. The "new world order" looks suspiciously like the old, with bombs and bullets doing all the talking.

I recall sometime in September reading an article in the New York Times that marveled at "the silence of the churches" over the Persian Gulf crisis. And there was, by and large, a remarkable silence. I think we were all pretty disoriented by the swiftness and unexpectedness of the events in the Gulf. Furthermore, what was there to protest? A brutal aggression against the small nation of Kuwait had taken place. Saudi Arabia seemed threatened and had a right to defend itself. Who could fault the United States and the larger United Nations for rushing to the defense of Saudi Arabia and for demanding that Iraq withdraw unconditionally? When the House of Bishops of the Episcopal Church met in late September, a resolution firmly supported the President of the United States in his actions in the Gulf.

But there were disturbing signs. In early October, I wrote a letter to Episcopalians expressing some of my own disquiet...

A previously silent church began to speak out, with remarkable unanimity. In November the National Conference of Catholic Bishops issued an analysis using the venerable Catholic tradition of "just war" theory. The bishops found that administration action "could well violate" just war criteria, especially in regard to proportionality of response and the criterion of last resort.

A few days later the General Board of the National Council of Churches deplored "reckless rhetoric" and "imprudent behavior" on the part of the administration and called for the immediate withdrawal of US troops, except those who might be required by a unified UN command.

At the same time the General Board was meeting in Portland, Oregon, heads of Protestant and Orthodox churches in the US with close partnership relations in the Middle East began to confer by conference call on a joint approach to President Bush. A letter was sent to the President on November 29th declaring flatly that these heads of churches would "oppose a unilateral use of military force" by Mr. Bush. These same church heads, joined by others in the National Council of Churches, embarked in early December on a Church Leaders' Peace Pilgrimage at the invitation of the Middle East Council of Churches. Visiting

Cyprus, Lebanon, Israel and the Occupied Territories, Jordan and Iraq, the religious leaders declared unanimously that war was "not the answer" to the Persian Gulf crisis, for war would only compound the tragedy and cause unspeakable destruction in the human, environmental and material fabric of already poor countries. On behalf of the religious leaders, I carried this message to the White House, where, on the day of our return from the Middle East, I met with President Bush and Secretary of State Baker.

The churches in the United States awakened from their slumber and passionately urged a negotiated political solution to the crisis. But the awakening was not without struggle. The struggle was, as always, to be faithful disciples of the Prince of Peace in a fallen and sinful world. On the one hand, we could not but condemn in the strongest possible terms the rape of Kuwait, and we could not but support the measured and nearly unanimous action of the United Nations in sanctioning the regime of Saddam Hussein. Nor could we but support our brave young men and women on the front lines, many of them victims of their own country's racial and economic injustices.

On the other hand, because of our close relations with brothers and sisters in the faith throughout the Middle East, and because of our justified suspicions of our own nation's mixed motives, we could not but protest mightily against the gathering storm of war and what we saw as tragedy compounded.

That struggle to fashion a witness faithful to the gospel of Jesus Christ has been a common element in the recent history of all the churches represented here tonight. We each have our own stories to tell—and we will tell them, here in this great gathering of Christians from around the world. My story differs only in the added detail that the President of the United States and the Secretary of State are both loyal and active members of the Episcopal Church. While some think I have been disloyal to our President, I believe I have kept faith with him. I have met and talked privately with the President twice since returning from the Middle East. Both he and I have been clear about our positions and both of us, I believe, have recognized that we each were acting in integrity and speaking as we had to speak. I could not live with myself had I not spoken as clearly as I could to our President and had I not done everything in my power to urge a negotiated political solution to the crisis. I pledge to continue strenuous peacemaking efforts in cooperation with all who seek to act in faith and refuse to give in to despair. Even in the heat of battle Christians are called to be peacemakers.

Remarks to General Convention, Phoenix, August 1991

Christians in the Middle East were heartened and given strength by the remarkably unified witness of our North American churches against the rush to war in the Persian Gulf. I know that for some of you it was difficult to see your Presiding Bishop in the forefront of such a witness. But it made a positive difference in the lives of our Middle Eastern sisters and brothers in the faith, particularly those of our own partner church in the Diocese of Jerusalem. Living in a largely Muslim world, often themselves held in suspicion by their neighbors, these Middle Eastern Christians were able to point to the voice of the church in the United States as a morally distinct voice, anchored in Christian faith and spoken from the freedom of a democratic environment. No witness from the West could have had a more positive evangelistic impact than this.

Comments at All Saints' Church, Pasadena, December 12, 1994

The war in the Persian Gulf showed that our lifestyle has come to depend on cheap oil. We lost sight of this underlying motive for this war in the fervor for patriotic zeal. But my real pain has been for the innocent who have suffered from this war, and for those who today are displaced by it. We are receiving reports that an estimated one million children have died in the aftermath of the Gulf War. I still wonder about the well-being of the little Iraqi girl I saw in the airport in Baghdad in 1990. War was not the answer.

Letter to President Clinton on Iraq sanctions, February 9, 1995, from Bishop Browning and Joan Campbell, General Secretary, National Council of Churches

Four years ago, we visited Iraq as members of a delegation of church leaders from the United States. Our visit took place only a few weeks before the onset of the Gulf War. We hoped that our witness for a peaceful resolution of the Gulf Crisis might prevent military action by the coalition forces.

Currently, four years after the war, the people of Iraq continue to face a battle—a battle against impoverishment and illness—as a result of the economic sanctions imposed on Iraq by the United Nations Security Council.

After numerous reports from reputable observers, including two assessments requested by UNICEF, as well as a visit to Iraq by a representative of our Church World Service and Witness Unit of the National Council of Churches, there is no doubt in our minds that the severe economic sanctions imposed against Iraq have caused enormous suffering among the civilian population. Food is in short supply, or is unaffordable. Iraq's medical system, once one of the best in the Middle East, is unable to function because medication and medical equipment are unavailable. The people most affected by these shortages are the most vulnerable—children, women, and the elderly.

There is no evidence that the ostensible target of the sanctions, the regime of President Saddam Hussein, has been significantly weakened. The Iraqi Army remains intact, and the secret police continue to terrorize people into quiet submission.

We acknowledge that Iraq has not complied fully with the conditions set forth in the cease-fire agreement, although it has made progress toward compliance. We also understand the risk that, even if economic sanctions are relaxed, the Iraqi government could misuse resources and withhold humanitarian supplies to its citizens. The current situation, however, must change. The sick and suffering people of Iraq have become victims of decisions made not only by their own government but by the United Nations, as well. The United States can take the first step toward ending this suffering by leading the Security Council to relax the sanctions against Iraq.

We regret very much the Security Council's recent decision to prolong this cruel punishment of an entire people, and that our own government has influenced this decision. We strongly urge the United Nations Security Council, and our representatives in that Council, to seek for a way to provide humanitarian relief to the Iraqi people. While the sanctions do not prohibit the importation of food or medicine, it is clear that international charitable efforts cannot meet the great needs of Iraq's population. The time has come for Iraq to be permitted to sell oil in order to feed and care for its own people.

We also believe that, in the long run, opening Iraq to the international community would be a greater threat to the regime's stability than prolonging the country's imposed isolation. Exposing Iraq to new ideas and to the promising democratic trends now beginning to appear in the Middle East would surely pose a significant danger to the suffocating rule of Saddam Hussein.

In a spirit of compassion toward the helpless and the innocent, we urge a relaxation of sanctions against the people of Iraq.

CENTRAL AMERICA AND PANAMA

While the entire Central America region was destabilized during the 1980's, the conflicts in El Salvador and Nicaragua were the most disturbing. Bishop Browning became deeply involved in those conflicts as well as Panamanian affairs where the US maintained such enormous influence.

Address to Executive Council, February 1986

To our sisters and brothers in Central America and Panama. I state today my firm support. On my first year's international agenda I hope to make a visit to this region to affirm this support. I want you to know personally of my commitment to you and to the self-determination of your dioceses and nations. As in South Africa and Namibia, I encourage us to see the root causes of suffering in Central America in its poverty and injustice, not in communism.

El Salvador

In 1986 the Civil War in El Salvador was at high intensity with the US supplying military and technical aid to the government. When ten humanitarian workers were arrested, Browning began his long and influential involvement in the conflict.

In 1989, nine Episcopal church workers and other denominational staff were arrested and Browning launched an exhausting effort to win their release. He urgently sought help from the new administration of George Bush, pointing out to him and Secretary of State James Baker, both Episcopalians, that nine of these church workers were members of their church. In early December, 1989, Browning led a delegation to a meeting with Bernard Aronson, Assistant

Secretary of State for Latin America, to express the churches' outrage. The State Department responded with a strong letter to President Cristiani threatening to cut off military aid if the attacks on the churches continued. Cristiani immediately issued an order and troops were withdrawn from church properties. Baker, in a meeting in January with Browning and other US religious leaders, urged them to meet with President Cristiani. Browning hosted a meeting with Cristiani at the Episcopal Church Center in New York January 31 at which Cristiani brought his cabinet and apologized for the attacks on church properties and vowed they would not occur again. This was the last incident of its kind. The workers were released a short time later.

The Episcopal Church's successful efforts were widely noted and the leadership of the Farubundo Marti Liberacion Nacional (FMLN)—the insurgency—asked Browning to deliver a peace proposal to the US government. He agreed and took a sealed envelope from the FMLN and placed it on the desk of Bernard Aronson in February. The envelope was at first refused, but Browning determinedly would not take it back, saying he brought it as a gesture of peace. Browning's backchannel connections to the FMLN continued during the course of peace negotiations which eventually culminated in a peace agreement brokered by the United Nations.

Letter to Salvadoran President José Napoleon Duarte, 1986

I write to you to express concern for the well-being of human rights and humanitarian workers in El Salvador. This concern is linked to the preservation of the due process of law and the protection of the innocent.

As the Primate and Chief Pastor of the Episcopal Church with episcopal authority for the Diocese of El Salvador, I write to express my deep and abiding concern at the news of the detention and public display of persons who have worked for humanitarian organizations. I write to urge you to take a personal interest in this situation and to use the authority of your office to insure that the physical safety and human rights of these detained persons are fully protected. The seriousness of public accusations against other church workers requires careful and impartial inquiry through the universally recognized legal procedures of jurisprudence which guarantee the protection of all innocent people.

I have a deep pastoral concern for all members of our Christian family in El Salvador who have served their country loyally and faithfully through their ministry to the many victims of civil strife and dislocation in El Salvador. They need your protection and the guarantee of a just legal process to insure that they have every opportunity to prove their innocence. The international Church community, which has supported them in their work, is keeping them in its prayers and intercessions.

As you know from our previous correspondence of our support for you and your family in the time of your great distress, and the visit with you of some of my staff, I have the deepest respect and regard for you and the leadership you are providing for El Salvador in these tense and difficult days. I was greatly encouraged when I heard that you had again resumed direct conversations for peace in El Salvador. You are in my prayers as you undertake this peacemaking process. I have every confidence that the Church organizations and Church workers in El Salvador will continue to give this difficult process their loyal support.

I will continue to keep you fully informed about the present situation and offer to support and assist you in ways you deem appropriate to uphold justice and the impartial process of the law in El Salvador.

Let My People Go, Pastoral letter, Christmas 1989

I greet you at this most holy of times as we celebrate once again the coming of the Prince of Peace.

This is a time when we lift up a message of hope for the whole world, a world that is shattered, and broken, but, in Christ, is also full of promise. We see encouraging signs from Eastern Europe, but we see also the continuing divisions between North and South. Parts of the world are celebrating and rejoicing in a new wave of freedom. Other parts of the world cry out in pain and anguish.

One of those cries of pain comes from El Salvador. I speak to you as the Presiding Bishop and primate for the region of all the United States and Central America. Despite every effort that I and countless other Episcopalians have made these past few weeks, nine Episcopal church workers are being held captive in El Salvador, including Father Luis Serrano. They are being held by the same forces that are the prime suspects in the death of six Jesuit priests. I fear for their safety and I fear for their lives.

The charges against them are totally false and without grounds. I say this confidently and without hesitation. Their only crime is to have befriended the poor and supported their cause for peace with justice.

As Moses said to Pharaoh, "Let my people go," so I am moved to say to the government of El Salvador, "Let our people go."

My friends, our church workers in El Salvador need our prayers at this hour. They also need us to lift our voices to the halls of government in Washington and El Salvador. I ask you to make a witness at this time of expectation and hope. Carry the message of the Prince of Peace to those accountable for the heinous actions against our people. Join with me and tell the President of El Salvador to let our people go.

Speak also to our president and your Congressional representatives as well. As long as our government continues to give $1.5 million a day to the government of El Salvador, our country is blessing the persecution of the churches. Let the message be—no more funding until all our people are released, the campaign of persecution is ended, the death squads are disbanded, the murderers of the Jesuit priests and two women are brought to justice, a ceasefire is in place and a process for peace is seriously engaged.

May the Prince of Peace be a light in the darkness and a beacon of hope for a weary world. God bless each of you. Pray for me as I pray for you.

Statement on El Salvador's Commission on Truth report, March 24, 1993

As we remember today the martyrdom of Oscar Romero, one of the thousands of Salvadorans murdered during years of civil war, we can look to the report of the Truth Commission as a vindication that truth can be more powerful than bullets and death squads.

The report is a beacon. I hope it will stand as a model to the world and let all brutal regimes know that we will never rest until the truth is told and the horrors exposed and the guilty brought to justice.

How shameful it is that the United States, the world's champion of democracy, provided the weapons for this slaughter and the training for the perpetrators of these heinous crimes. Our national character is badly damaged. No amount of economic aid can ever make up for what we contributed to this disgrace of history. But we must in every way contribute to the economic rebuilding of this new and peaceful democracy.

But before serious economic development can take place, the recommendations of the Truth Commission report must be fully implemented. The amnesty decision of the Salvadoran government cannot stand. On this day, the anniversary of the martyrdom of Archbishop Romero, I call upon the international community to apply all appropriate pressure to finish the task and to see that those responsible for the atrocities on both sides of the conflict are purged and brought to true justice in a re-formed judiciary. I applaud the call by Congressmen Serrano and McDermott for full compliance. And for the sake of our own national soul, I call for an investigation, and where appro-priate, prosecution of US officials involved in lying to Congress and covering up these atrocities.

Nicaragua

The Contra war in Nicaragua opened a deep rift between mainline churches and the Reagan administration. A letter to Reagan was given short shrift by the administration. Browning led a visit of four Anglican primates to Nicaragua and Panama in 1989 as a response to his deep concerns for that region.

Text of letter to President Reagan, 1986

I write regarding your proposed financial and moral sup-port of the "Contra" forces against the government of Nicaragua. The five Episcopal Dioceses of Central America are a part of the Episcopal Church. We are proud of the mission and minis-try of our sisters and brothers in Central America and we support them and their leadership . . .

After a two-year process, including a series of extensive visitations . . . the General Convention of the Episcopal Church, meeting in Anaheim, California, in September, 1985, passed two resolutions opposing *all* covert aid to the "Contras and at-tempts to destabilize the government of Nicaragua . . ."

On a personal note, Mr. President, I must share with you

that I have several disquieting questions about your policies and your characterizations of some of the governments in Central America, and political processes and conditions in the region; and, I must admit, some of your public statements about those in this country who do not share your perceptions.

It is less than helpful for our national leaders to coin or corrupt the language of our democracy in support of questionable foreign military forces. Identifying the "Contras" as "freedom fighters" obscures the issues in an attempt to attach the "Contras" to the historic memory of the US.

To disregard the reports of reputable international human rights agencies or undermine their credibility and legitimacy by preemptive accusations of "a disinformation campaign" does not seem to serve the interests of our national decision-making process, serve the interests of those in legitimate need, nor enhance the vital work of independent, international human rights agencies and advocates.

Statement of Anglican Bishops and Archbishops on Nicaragua, March 18, 1989

We are a delegation of Anglican Primates and the President of the IXth Province of the Episcopal Church in the United States. We have come to Nicaragua at the invitation of our brother, the Bishop of Nicaragua, Sturdie W. Downs, to share in a ministry and witness to the people of God in this country of much suffering. We have come with the hope that our visit will enable us to become advocates for justice which will bear fruit in a lasting peace and that we may be an encouragement to the Nicaraguan Church as it ministers to a long-suffering people . . .

To aid in our understanding, we have met with people representative of the entire political spectrum including the Independent Human Rights Group; the government's human rights group; representatives of the ecumenical community—CEPAD and CEBIC; the editors of three major dailies. We also met with civic and diplomatic officials including the President, the Vice President, the Mayor of Bluefields, a representative to the National Assembly from the Atlantic Coast region, and the Charge d'Affaire at the United States Embassy. Our visit was strengthened by many face-to-face contacts with the Nicaraguan people both within and without the Anglican community. As a delegation of Christian leaders, we regret that Cardinal Obando y Bravo was unable to see us.

It is significant to note that we come at the beginning of Passiontide, the most sacred period of our church calendar. This was not an accident. The Nicaraguan people have described their life and spiritual journey as a constant passion—they live each day as a *via crucis*. Our presence is a show of solidarity and a demonstration of a faith in a loving and reconciling God.

One cannot visit the country without being overwhelmed by the toll on life and property caused by a chain of events—the oppression of the Somoza regime, earthquake, hurricane, and agonizing civil war, and forest fires—to name the most devastating. We are especially moved by the enormity of the destruction on the Atlantic Coast—in Bluefields. The suffering of mothers who have lost their children, children who have lost their parents, families divided through civil strife is all too apparent.

Nicaragua suffers from the international debt crisis affecting many Latin American and other developing nations. This economic crisis has been exacerbated by the direction of resources to the Civil War and the recent devastation of the environment caused by Hurricane Joan.

We have, during our visit, felt deep distress and anger when we have seen the intense suffering inflicted on the people of Nicaragua by the "contra" war—a war financed and sponsored by people sitting in the safety of foreign capitals. Our Nicaraguan experience has given us a new sympathy for the view of great numbers of people in the developing world that United

States administrations, in this case, the Reagan administration, have been prepared to subject entire peoples to the ravages of war to pursue their economic interests and because of objections to the ideological complexion of their governments. We have heard the United States government justify its refusal to impose further sanctions against apartheid in South Africa on the grounds that they would cause suffering. We find this argument to be in total conflict with the United States government's willingness to impose sanctions on Nicaragua and Panama and to inflict the evil of war on the people of Nicaragua. It is our hope that the new Bush administration and policies emerging therefrom will open a window of opportunity for change.

The five Central American presidents, representing governments of a wide range of political persuasions, took a step of great importance when, following up their earlier initiatives, they signed the agreement of February 14, in El Salvador. We admire the willingness of President Ortega, for whatever reason, to allow specific focus on the problems of his country in that agreement. The actions of the Nicaraguan government since the agreement, in particular the release of political prisoners, appear to us to demonstrate a commitment to allowing freer political activity and to bringing about peace based on reconciliation. We appeal to the Nicaraguan government to follow up this week's amnesty by releasing all prisoners falling within the classification made by the Inter-American Human Rights Commission.

We have no doubt the vast majority of Nicaraguans want an end to foreign sponsorship of conflict in their country, and we support unequivocally the request of the Central American presidents that governments within and outside the region should immediately cease aid to irregular or insurrectional forces. In response to the recent proposals of the United States administration for new aid to contra forces in Honduras, we can accept such aid only if it contributed directly to the implementation of the El Salvador agreement. There must be enforceable guarantees that aid is used for repatriating members of the contra forces or relocating them in third countries. We reject any suggestion that humanitarian assistance should be used to keep them in Honduras as a threat hanging over the head of the Sandinista government.

We affirm the right of the region to determine its own future. We urge the governments of North America and Europe to support the implementation by Central American nations of the Esquipulus II peace process. We are aware of the invitation to the government of Canada from the Central American nations to participate in the international, unarmed verification team called for by the Esquipulus II peace accord, and we urge the government to respond positively.

We are encouraged by the decision of Nicaragua's National Reconciliation Commission to send a delegation to contra camps in Honduras to investigate the whereabouts of children allegedly kidnaped by the counterrevolutionary forces, and will call on the contras to return the children. We urge the Honduran government to facilitate the process.

We have heard reports from human rights agencies in Nicaragua that have documented abuses and violations committed by both the Sandinista government and the counterrevolutionary forces. We denounce all such violations and urge both the government and the contra forces to respect the basic human rights of the people of Nicaragua.

Our witness to Nicaragua's physical devastation causes us to urge our governments to respond to the overwhelming need for development assistance, especially in the Atlantic Coast area where reconstruction assistance is needed to aid in the recovery from the effects of Hurricane Joan.

We support the prophetic witness of the Episcopal Church in Nicaragua and that of the ecumenical community in their efforts to be peacemakers and reconcilers, and we will urge our churches to be fully supportive of the Episcopal Church and its mission and ministry.

The Most Rev. Edmond L. Browning, United States

The Most Rev. Orlando U. Lindsay, West Indies

The Most Rev. Michael Peers, Canada

The Most Rev. Desmond M. Tutu, Southern Africa

The Rt. Rev. James H. Ottley, Bishop of Panama

Panama

Panama was an issue of concern to Browning throughout his term because of US influence, but it was the invasion in December 1989 that he came to deeply regret.

Statement of Anglican primates on Panama, March 20, 1989

We are a delegation of Anglican Primates who are making a pastoral visit in the Diocese of Panama at the invitation of the Episcopal Bishop, James H. Ottley. Bishop Ottley invited us to the Diocese at the conclusion of our pastoral visit in the Diocese of Nicaragua . . .

From our two-day visit, we would like to address these specific concerns: human rights, the May 7 election, sanctions and . . . the role of the Church.

We have been informed by various groups and organizations of the disastrous effects of the US sanctions against Panama. These sanctions have led to the destruction of the country's economy, caused immense suffering on the poorest of the poor, increased unemployment, and aggravated social problems. It is also apparent to us that the government of Panama uses the effect of these sanctions to rally nationalist support against the United States. This paralyzes many people who, like the majority of Panamanians, are opposed to sanctions, but who are restricted from speaking out on this issue for fear of being labeled in favor of General Noriega. We can therefore say that these sanctions inflict a double oppression on the citizens of Panama.

We believe that these sanctions, opposed by the general population, and inflicted by the United States in an attempt to force the ouster of General Noriega, must cease. The US policy has failed, and their continued imposition helps the government to direct attention from the real, serious internal economic and political crisis. We call upon the US government, therefore, to immediately end the sanctions placed on Panama, so that the unjust suffering can be alleviated and so that the overwhelming domestic problems can be brought to light and addressed by the people of Panama, as a sovereign independent nation, without external oppression and interferences.

During our visit, we heard allegations of serious human rights abuses perpetrated by the government. We were told that political prisoners were being held in jail without trial, specifically that soldiers accused of trying to overthrow General Noriega had been jailed for more than a year. We also heard of activists being forced to leave the country and go into exile. We call for the release of prisoners held without trial and for an end to persecution of opposition party members . . .

We commend the holding of the general elections set for May 7, 1989. They are a sign of hope for the society, and the fact that all Panamanians have been promised the right to vote is one of the reasons we can oppose the implementation of sanctions on Panama while supporting them against apartheid in South Africa.

However, their legitimacy will be open to question both in Panama and in the international community if they are conducted with the media restricted and in the absence of credible international observers. We therefore urge the government of Panama to lift all restrictions on the media with immediate effect. We further request the Electoral Court to allow observers from different international organizations to guarantee just elections. Arising from discussions at our meeting with General Noriega, we as Primates of the Anglican Communion intend on asking the world church community to appoint a delegation of election observers to travel to Panama and observe the elections on our behalf. We finally issue an appeal for the results of just elections to be respected as the will of the people of Panama . . .

We have visited with the churches and heard their concerns and hope and agreed that, if the Church is to bring about reconciliation and peace between brothers and sisters in Panama, between opposition and government differences, it is necessary to work without taking partisan positions in the political arena. Trust needs to be planted, so that reconciliation can be attained.

Therefore, as Primates of the Anglican Communion visiting Panama March 19-21, 1989, we commend and encourage the work being done by the Christian Churches together in their effort to attain this reconciliation and peace among the Panamanian family, and we will urge our churches to be fully supportive of the Episcopal Church in the Diocese of Panama in its mission and ministry.

The Most Rev. Edmond L. Browning, United States

The Most Rev. Orland U. Lindsay, West Indies

The Most Rev. Michael Peers, Canada

The Most Rev. Desmond M. Tutu, Southern Africa

Statement on Panama at the time of the US invasion, December 21, 1989

I have been in touch with the Diocese of Panama and determined that Bishop Ottley, his family and staff are safe and unharmed. I have not yet been able to speak personally with Bishop Ottley because of downed telephone communications. As far as we know, no members of the diocese have been harmed. American missionaries are unharmed. I look forward to speaking with the Bishop as soon as possible. Until that time, I can only say that I am profoundly saddened that the Administration has found it necessary to intervene militarily and unilaterally once again in the affairs of a Western hemisphere nation—even in the face of extreme provocation. Though I admit to some mixed feelings at the moment, I cannot believe that such a violent act will issue in a just solution. I mourn the deaths both of US soldiers and civilians and of Panamanian citizens. The Christmas worship of our people must bear eloquent testimony to the only enduring solution to the tragedies of this world: the sacrificial and forbearing love of the Prince of Peace.

THE CARIBBEAN
Haiti—The overthrow of Aristide

The church has learned that sanctions are not always the answer to violence in opposing tyranny. This became clear to the Presiding Bishop, first in Iraq, then in Haiti. While they were the tool that brought down apartheid, they didn't work for restoring democracy in Haiti, in large measure because they were unevenly applied.

During staff discussions with the Presiding Bishop, there was general agreement that US policy in Latin America and the Caribbean had always been jingoistic and, even with the overthrow of President Aristide, was likely to lean to what would benefit US corporate interests, not democracy or human rights. This made any idea of a US invasion to restore Aristide anathema. But after Clinton came to office and the Congressional black caucus leaned on him to make a military response against the dictators, Browning began to rethink his position. The driving impetus behind his thinking was to end the suffering of the Haitian people which pained him personally. Sanctions were hurting them, not the dictators. Hours before the US was to invade Haiti in September, 1994, the military junta surrended power and the invasion was avoided.

During Aristide's exile in the United States, he paid a visit to the Presiding Bishop and the Church Center in New York. A moving moment occurred when time was arranged for Haitian staff, about six of them, to meet privately with Aristide. One of them, a night custodian, donned a suit and said proudly afterwards, "I met my president today."

Statement on Haiti, November 1, 1993

The deterioration of the situation in Haiti compels a response from all people of conscience. Every death is a tragedy, every act of terror a betrayal and every broken promise a cry to the world to stop the carnage.

The failure of the Haitian military to live up to the Governor's Island agreement to allow the return of Haiti's legitimately elected president, Jean Bertrand Aristide, lays bare the evil of that illegitimate regime and its hired guns.

I utterly deplore the nefarious accusations by the CIA being leveled at President Aristide's commitment to democracy and his competence to hold office. Such accusations, coming as they do now, undermine the democratic process and give aid and comfort to those now terrorizing the Haitian people.

Therefore, I support the reimposed oil and arms embargo by the United Nations (provided humanitarian goods be exempted) and the blockade enforcing it, and I support the suspension of visas and the freezing of assets ordered by President Bill Clinton.

Further, until democracy is restored and President Aristide returned to his rightful place, I call upon President Clinton and the United Nations to consider the following additional actions:

■ Use all diplomatic means to insure that the neighboring Dominican Republic observe the embargo and prevent goods leaking across its border or face sanctions itself.

- End immediately by executive order the interdiction and repatriation of Haitian refugees and make preparation to welcome and resettle those who escape.

- Increase the freeze on assets and suspension of visas to all 200 military officers, the industrialists who support them and the members of their families. Deport immediately all those now living in the United States (including their college-enrolled children) and ask our allies to do the same.

The October 30 date for President Aristide's return has passed. But that date serves as an important symbol for the millions of Haitian citizens who voted for him, support him and want him back. We cannot let them down.

Statement on Haiti, July 15, 1994

Like many Americans, I am outraged at the continuing impasse over the return to democracy in Haiti. The recent expulsion of international human rights monitors is yet another sign of the utter corruption of the Haitian government. The failure to implement the UN brokered Governor's Island agreement last October remains an embarrassment to us all. After months of faltering and sometimes encouraging steps by the international community, we are haunted by the continuing specter of terror against the Haitian people every day by a military regime of despotic thugs.

My deepest embarrassment, however, is over the way our government has fumbled the issue of Haitian refugees. Let me say it the way I see it. Our policy is sheer racism and is a blight on our best instincts as Americans to embrace refugees. We ourselves have forgotten our roots and our own struggle for democracy and freedom.

I am grateful to a delegation to Haiti on my behalf led by the Honorable David Dinkins this past June 2-5. In their report they say: "If military action is to be contemplated, it should be multi-national." I know this advice was not made lightly.

I absolutely abhor the thought of the United States invading yet another Latin American/Caribbean nation. I do not see how we can do so again in Haiti without remembering our interventionist past in that island country. It is clear from history that the terroristic state of Haiti today owes part of its existence to the legacy of past US policy. We are deeply complicit. Can we, therefore, mount a unilateral invasion and have credibility that we are genuinely promoting democracy?

Yet I am anxious to see the end of suffering in Haiti as quickly as possible. If the only means to end this nightmare for the people of Haiti is through military intervention, then let it be led by multi-lateral forces. Only an international response, and not the US alone, can hold out the hope of a genuine mission to restore democracy to Haiti.

Until such a multi-lateral effort is undertaken, I beseech my government, in the name of all that is decent, to lead other nations in receiving those beleaguered Haitians who risk their lives to come to America. The Episcopal Church stands ready to do its part through our Episcopal Migration Ministries office and I urge our Central American/Panama bishops to support safe haven in their countries as well. Every Haitian refused is a blot on our collective conscience.

Cuba

Bishop Browning's visit to Cuba in March of 1996 was the first by a Presiding Bishop since Castro came to power in 1959. Just prior to that visit, the Cuban military had shot down two airplanes flown by Cuban Americans near or in

Cuban airspace. This prompted a tightening of the US embargo on Cuba with the passage of the Helms-Burton Act. Browning responded by asking the President to waive a key provision in the new law.

Letter to President Clinton, July 9, 1996

I urge you to waive implementation of Title III of the Cuba Liberty and Democratic Solidarity Act. As you know, Title III allows US citizens to sue foreign corporations that allegedly benefit from properties expropriated by the Cuban government. This provision not only violates international law and antagonizes US partners abroad, it symbolizes a deep deterioration of US-Cuba relations. Thirty years of an embargo and isolation has not produced the kind of change that serves the interest of the United States or the people of Cuba. I urge you to encourage greater dialogue and peaceful change in Cuba, not further separation and antagonism between the two countries.

I visited the Episcopal Church of Cuba in March, 1996, soon after the shootdown of two US civilian aircraft on February 24. This was the first primatial and pastoral visit to the Cuban Church by a US Presiding Bishop since 1954. I returned with a renewed and strengthened conviction that only constructive engagement between the United States and Cuba will lead to more peaceful and democratic leadership in Cuba. I heard clearly from Episcopalians in Cuba of their desire for reconciliation within their country and with their brothers and sisters in exile who oppose Cuba's political regime.

Soon after my trip, the Episcopal Church in the US pledged to actively encourage greater dialogue and religious and cultural exchanges between the US and Cuba. The Church's Executive Council voted to urge Episcopalians and Episcopal organizations to respond to the invitation of the Diocese of Cuba to regularly send delegations to Cuba, and to invite Cuban Episcopalians to the United States.

I understand your outrage, and that of so many others in Congress and around the country, toward Cuba's downing of two US civilian aircraft on February 24. The Helms-Burton law has sent a clear message, in both real and symbolic ways, to Cuba's government that the US will not stand for such behavior. Title III, on the other hand, would punish our international partners and lead to further antagonism with Cuba. Such antagonism has proven over the years not to lead to democracy in Cuba. In fact, our Cuban brothers and sisters believe such actions only further embolden Cuba's regime.

The Episcopal Church is willing to do what it can to improve relations with Cuba. I hope you will do the same by using your authority to waive Title III.

ASIA
China

The television coverage of the events at Tienanmen Square are forever etched in the minds of those who saw them. As the crisis unfolded, Bishop Browning reached out to Christian counterparts in China.

Letter to K.H. Ting, President of the China Christian Council and an Anglican bishop, May 22, 1989

At this grave hour, I am writing to express the support and prayers of your brothers and sisters in the United States. I want you to know that we hold the welfare and security of those pressing for democratic reforms and those responsible for bringing a peaceful resolution to the current situation in our prayers. May you be strengthened to meet the extraordinary demands that these troubled times are placing on you.

If I can be of any assistance to you during this time, please do not hesitate to reach out. Patti joins me in sending this message of support and tribute.

May our Risen Lord give you the strength to lead your people through to safety and justice.

Statement on China, June 8, 1989

I know that you all are concerned for the people of China and the Church there. This is to inform you of the actions we have taken on your behalf.

Today, in the name of the Episcopal Church, I have written to The China Christian Council expressing our sorrow, solidarity and support for the people and Church in China in this time of deep crisis.

A crisis team has been constituted at the Episcopal Church Center to monitor the developments in China and to frame an appropriate strategy for Episcopal Church response through your Presiding Bishop . . .

We are maintaining contact with the China Program of the National Council of Churches and the Amity Foundation in China, through which we have two persons serving in China. At this time we have been assured of their safety and their desire to remain there.

I earlier expressed our support directly to Bishop K.H. Ting, President of the China Christian Council, for his courageous statement of solidarity with the democracy movement led by the students, including Christian seminarians.

Each of us in the Episcopal Church in the United States has an important contribution to make. I call on the clergy and people for their continued prayers for the victims of the recent violence and those who mourn; for the people and for the church of China; and for those who must make the fateful decisions concerning the future of that nation.

May the Holy Spirit unite us in hope with those who struggle for justice and peace in China and throughout the world.

The Philippines

Beginning in 1990, the Presiding Bishop began a quiet diplomatic effort with the US government in response to a request from the Episcopal Church in the Philippines. The Philippines has been in the midst of an insurgency by the New Peoples Army since 1967. Much of the conflict, while nationwide, has centered in northern Luzon where the Episcopal Church has its strongest presence. The church suffered badly for its witness for justice, often being harassed and threatened by government troops. A number of civilian members of the church were killed in the conflict and church members served on both sides.

Churches took a prominent role beginning in the 1980's to promote a peace process between the government and the political wing of the New Peoples Army, the National Democratic Front. The Presiding Bishop agreed to meet with US leaders and NDF officials to encourage US support for both sides in the conflict to move from a policy of war to a policy of peace.

The efforts to encourage the peace process continued throughout Bishop Browning's term with both sides to the conflict engaged in tortuous peace talks in the Netherlands.

Letter to James Baker, Secretary of State, December 13, 1991

I come to you today at the urgent request of our partner Churches in the Philippines.

Mr. Secretary, my plea is that you sever all United States relations with the "total war" policy of the Philippines and to seek through your good office actions to promote a peace process.

Our partner Church, the Philippine Episcopal Church, is under assault. I share with you today a resolution of our Northern Philippines Diocese calling on President Aquino to withdraw armed forces from the Mountain Province. This military build-up is taking place in the very heart of the Episcopal Church.

The Marag Valley in Northern Luzon has been under siege for several months. This is in another populated Episcopal diocese. Philippine Churches have been stopped from conducting mercy missions to civilian victims. Gross human rights abuses by government troops are being reported by our Church workers.

It is my understanding the Philippine government is determined to escalate its "total war" policy with tactical, financial and advisory support from the United States.

At the behest of Church leadership in the Philippines, I met with National Democratic Front officials on December 2 in Toronto to prepare for this meeting with you. I want to share a letter they have written to me. Clearly, they know the problems of the Philippines cannot be resolved militarily. We, too, need to recognize that a just peace cannot come to the Philippines through napalm and brutal military offensives.

I ask today that you take a leap of faith with me and give diplomacy and negotiations a chance. Two years ago you set in motion a peace process for ending the war in El Salvador. You are today a tireless champion for peace in the Middle East. Now, I ask you to be a peacemaker for the Philippines.

I want to be very specific. I ask you to consider the following steps to move from a policy of war to a policy of peace:

a.   Use the influence of your good office to persuade President Aquino to support a peace process without preconditions. She has agreed to hold similar talks with the Moro National Liberation Front under the auspices of the Islamic Conference. A public announcement from President Aquino to extend the traditional Christmas and New Year's cease fire would be an excellent signal, followed by an announcement to send an authorized delegation to begin serious and substantive talks with the NDF at an agreed site overseas.

b.   Postpone indefinitely US delivery of 19 OV 10 Bronco aircraft pending a review of the "total war" policy. I am pained to learn that we have already sent five of these aircraft to the AFP that will surely lead to much death and destruction among the poorest of the Philippine community.

These two steps would be dramatic and welcome evidence of a humane approach to resolving this long and protracted struggle . . .

There is yet another request I would make of you today. Undertake a review of the policy listing the NDF, the Communist Party of the Philippines and the New Peoples Army as terrorist organizations . . .

The designation of "terrorist" does not serve a peace process. I know that Americans have been killed in this conflict because of our role in supporting counterinsurgency. But the same was true in El Salvador, and yet the FMLN had an active presence in the United States. Our partner churches in the Philippines complain far more about "terrorist" acts by government forces than from the New Peoples Army. This experience is confirmed in reports of human rights organizations, including Amnesty International. A review of our policy is very much in order . . .

Finally, I offer the full weight of my office in support of this peace effort. I am willing to communicate and mediate with all parties, including the National Democratic Front, if that will further the cause of peace.

Letter to James Baker, Secretary of State, December 17, 1991

I could not be more grateful for your willingness to take precious time to allow me the opportunity to present my concerns for a peace process in the Philippines. And I look forward to your response to my suggestions which I left with Mr. Solomon.

The cause of peace is always worth the effort, and I believe there is a very real chance of peace for the Philippines if we have but the will. I want you to know I am joined to this effort with our partner Churches for the long haul.

Terrorism is a terrible scourge. And the killing of Americans is a terrible thing. So is the taking of human life whether American or Filipino. I want to see the end of this human suffering as soon as possible. And you, good sir, can provide the key to start the process.

That is why I was so heartened to hear your willingness to entertain ideas for getting the two sides to the peace table. I will certainly convey to the authorized leadership of the National Democratic Front the deep concerns you expressed. I believe their desire for a just peace is genuine, and, while the differences between the two sides may be wide, they are not irreconcilable.

The long war in El Salvador seemed to be intractable only a short time ago. But through your good office a process for peace is at an advanced stage today.

Time is not a luxury in this matter. The violence is escalating and that inevitably translates into loss of life, pain, misery and grief. In the midst of everything else you do, I thank you for your efforts for peace in the Philippines.

Letter to Warren Christopher, Secretary of State, July 26, 1993

Today I want to follow up on the meeting with your Philippine office director, Mr. Timberlake Foster. Let me say at the outset how grateful I am to Mr. Foster for his generous time. I had with me Bishop Robert Longid of the Diocese of Northern Philippines. This was a valuable opportunity for him to discuss the very important efforts now under way to support a legitimate peace process in the Philippines . . .

There is in this process an appropriate role for the United States. Unfortunately, the role being played at this time does not bode well for the future of the peace process.

Mr. Foster made clear in his opening remarks that the policy outlined to me by Secretary Baker in December of 1991 is the same policy today. That policy provides material and technical support to the Armed Forces of the Philippines in its conduct of total war against the NPA with a timetable to win that war by December 31 of this year, extended since the original date for success in June 1992. That policy also labels the NPA a terrorist organization that targets Americans. The policy is based on support for a democratic government.

I am asking you today to explore new possibilities for American policy in the Philippines. While I applaud and support in every way our country's commitment to democracy, I would also like to see the Clinton Administration's commitment to human rights, environment and sustainable development applied to the Philippines.

The Philippine government has failed both under Mrs. Aquino and Mr. Ramos to address the massive poverty of the country or to eradicate human rights abuses from its military and para-military ranks. Nor has it significantly stemmed the gross injustices against the environment from such industries as logging. Nor has it been able to resolve the long-standing social problems of land distribution, and the government continues to be dogged by corruption and graft among its various branches, including in the national police.

All of these ills have combined over the course of this century to result in a deplorable tragedy of social and economic injustice in the Philippines, created under US colonial rule and post-colonial influence. The result is a civil war lasting twenty-four years and counting.

We can and should do so much better. The current peace

process cannot succeed unless the peace process seriously addresses the root causes of the conflict. I have doubts about the seriousness of present initiatives by President Ramos because while he talks peace, he wages total war and increases military spending.

I am writing to you today to ask that you make a review of current policy in the Philippines with specific intent to support an end to this long conflict based on negotiations which address root causes of the conflict. Conversely, I ask for reconsideration of existing policy which pursues a military solution to what are really social, economic and environmental problems.

Let me be clear that our role is not to impose a solution upon the Philippines. We have done that to the detriment of Filipinos for too long. Filipinos must resolve the issues that have caused civil war all these years.

What we can do, appropriately, is to support the peace process and encourage the two sides to negotiate their issues. We can also show that support by declining to participate in the policy of total war which leaves misery and suffering in its wake. Any policy that believes the conflict can be resolved militarily while root causes go unresolved is simply wrong. A policy of winning needs to give way to a policy of justice.

While I would expect our government to respect the legitimacy of the present Philippine administration, I also believe we could take a more balanced approach to the National Democratic Front.

I have discussed the issue of targeting Americans with the NDF for nearly two years, most recently dispatching my peace and justice officer to the Netherlands June 28. As long as the United States continues its support, both materially and technically, for the policy of total war, the NDF has said to me that it would be difficult to make a public declaration that it does not any longer have a policy that targets Americans.

However, the NDF has assured me that there are no intentions to carry out any actions against Americans and, in effect, there is no longer any such policy, evidenced by some three years since any incidents have occurred where an American life was taken. In fact, the NDF points out, the NPA released an American hostage at the request of myself and others last year.

I fully realize that the NDF has internal problems which question its cohesion and viability. But I think it would be a terrible mistake to believe that the NPA/NDF can be defeated militarily or by ignoring it. There will always be a basis for revolution as long as root causes are not addressed through serious negotiations.

I believe we might signal our good intentions through a number of possible moves. Certainly, a public statement supporting a serious peace process is one. Backing away from our role in total war would be another. Taking responsibility for cleaning up Subic Bay would be yet another. Such actions would demonstrate that the Clinton Administration's campaign themes are at work in the State Department . . .

We owe it to ourselves to do so as a nation that takes pride in its commitment to justice and freedom. And we certainly owe it to the Filipinos who have borne the brunt of so many of our mistakes.

Japan

In 1995, US military bases on Okinawa received intense media exposure when three American servicemen abducted and raped a twelve-year-old Okinawan girl. The peace and justice committee of the Nippon Sei Ko Kai (NSKK—Anglican Church in Japan), issued a strongly worded statement on September 30, 1995, against the presence of the bases and urged the Presiding Bishop to communicate its concern to President Clinton. In June of 1996 the Presiding Bishop sent a three-person delegation to Okinawa at the invitation of

the NSKK to make a pastoral and fact-finding visit. He also scheduled a visit for himself in May 1997.

Letter to President Clinton, November 15, 1995

I am passing on to you this day a message from the justice and peace committee of the Anglican Church in Japan. As you are well aware, and as is clear from the statement, there is great distress over the continuing presence of US military bases in Okinawa in the wake of the rape of a twelve year old student by US soldiers.

The Nippon Sei Ko Kai (Anglican Church in Japan) is a very important partner of the Episcopal Church USA, and we have recently begun discussions about the relationship of our Church to the Church in Okinawa. This is a matter I know a little something about as I served the diocese of Okinawa as priest and bishop in the 60's and early 70's.

I think this recent tragedy in Okinawa, combined with the 50th anniversary of the end of World War II, might be occasions for our government to re-think its long time security agreements in Japan. And I believe it would be encouraging to the people of Okinawa to have you call for a review of our presence there. I realize this may well run counter to current thinking, but I believe if we are to show genuine respect for the integrity of Okinawans, such a review is necessary.

Burma

The Presiding Bishop made a primatial visit to Burma (now known as Myanmar) in January 1996. Burma was under the military rule of SLORC, one of the most notorious regimes in the world. During his visit, Browning called on the Nobel Peace Prize laureate, Aung San Suu Kyi, leader of Burma's democracy movement. Reprisals by the military against visitors to Suu Kyi were always a worry and Suu

Kyi noted that Browning's and Burma's Anglican Archbishop's visit was the first by Christian leaders since her release from house arrest. "I am puzzled," she said, "why others haven't been before because I understand that Christians believe they have no one to fear but God."

Letter to several members of Congress and President Clinton, March 1996

I am anxious to take a few moments to share with you that I have recently returned from a visit to Burma . . . January 12-17, 1996, and included a visit with Aung San Suu Kyi. I also was hosted at a delightful dinner by *charges 'd affaires* Marilyn Myers . . .

While the purpose of the trip was to make a pastoral visit to our Church there, I could not escape seeing the harsh realities of life under the SLORC government which makes life so difficult for the Church as well as the general population. As one person said, there are no real laws to be broken in Burma because SLORC makes up its own laws to suit its own purposes on any given day. People live under a constant climate of fear. There are no human rights.

I am well aware that you know of the deplorable conditions existing in Burma today. I simply want to encourage all efforts of our country to convince SLORC that the restoration of democracy is the only way to economically develop the future of the country. I would be chagrined to see any US based investments there that would give aid and comfort to the regime. Let me say that I appreciate the recent and consistent position of our government in relation to Burma.

I found Aung San Suu Kyi strong and resolute during a one-hour meeting. I believe she was appreciative to receive support from a Christian source and was glad to hear of Churches working on behalf of human rights in Burma through the Interfaith Center for Corporate Responsibility in New York, among others. Aung San Suu Kyi is a courageous leader who needs the support of the international community.

Many of our Anglicans in Burma belong to ethnic minorities, especially the Karens, who are engaged in a 47-year-old civil war with the government. I met with a number of Anglican refugees in Bangkok before proceeding to Rangoon. Aung San Suu Kyi was very open to a just and fair solution for all the ethnic groups in Burma who feel so betrayed by events since the British withdrawal from the country after World War II.

I am enclosing articles prepared by our news department in the wake of the trip. Please know that I stand ready to assist you and our government in any way that might be helpful in promoting democracy and human rights in Burma and justice for its ethnic peoples. This comes with my warmest best wishes.

EUROPE

Bosnia-Herzegovina

Perhaps the most vexing issue to address in the Browning years was that of the war in the Balkans. The Presiding Bishop was faced with terribly difficult moral choices. And he agonized with staff about determining the fine line between the risk of widening the conflict and taking military action to stop it.

The phrase "humanitarian intervention" came into use as part of the post cold war vocabulary. The threat of nuclear war was greatly lessened, but more conventional conflicts ignited a new debate on the use of international forces to prevent or lessen the suffering of innocent people caught in the crossfire of ethnic and religious struggles. Was the right response a Vietnam, "it's-none-of-our-business" response, or a World War II "aggression-and-facism-must-be-

stopped" response?

As usual, Browning grappled with the issue and made his position clear, generally receiving praise for his leadership on such an agonizing subject. The only serious criticism he received came from the American Serbian community.

At one point during the Balkan conflict the Presiding Bishop sent an emissary to the Orthodox Patriarch of Moscow with a demarche for the patriarch to use his influence with the Serbian Orthodox to end the bloodshed. In response, the Patriarch issued a statement calling for an end to the violence. The Patriarch and the Presiding Bishop had met previously in both New York and Moscow.

Letter to President Bush, August 13, 1992

I wish to add my voice to the leadership of the National Council of Churches, the United Church of Christ and the Christian Church (Disciples of Christ) in expressing my dismay over the appalling tragedy which continues to unfold in Bosnia-Herzegovina.

I urge US support for the International Conference on Yugoslavia August 26-28 in London to be sponsored by the United Nations and the European Community. I ask that you also support "temporary protective status" to refugees from Bosnia and Herzegovina now in the US. In this spirit I ask that you grant the same status to Haitians fleeing persecution. This is our American tradition.

Statement on the situation in the former Yugoslavia, April 8, 1993

We seem to have moved a long way from the euphoria that accompanied the tearing down of the Berlin Wall. The sense of hope for a peaceful world that lifted our spirits then has faded into new questions about the brutal inhumanity we are witnessing in the former Yugoslavia.

That is not to say that we do not see atrocities elsewhere. They are all too present in every region of the globe—South Africa, Burma, Haiti, East Timor, Sri Lanka, Gaza and the West Bank, Cambodia, Bombay, Peru, Guatemala—and the litany goes on.

But Bosnia/Herzegovina has caused as deep an outcry of dismay and outrage as any I have heard since becoming Presiding Bishop. While other outrages are equally deserving of our dismay, for many Americans and Europeans, it reflects the shattering of a peace that was promised with the destruction of the Berlin Wall.

I am among those who have wrung their hands and deplored the violence and suffering. But I do not think our hand-wringing will be judged well by history.

The church's place is to speak to the deep moral issues of our time and to champion the cause of human rights and to respect, as we so often say at baptism, the dignity of every human being. In doing so, we have taken to the high moral ground of seeking peace through negotiation, reason and diplomacy—and without resort to arms.

And yet, ironically, we find that religion itself is a major contributor to the suffering today in the Balkans. People of two great branches of Christianity and a Muslim population vilify one another while the leadership of the churches is unable to stop the hatred and fighting. This makes Bosnia/Herzegovina a special challenge to the churches.

Those of us who opposed the Gulf War believed, I think correctly, that war was not the answer. But today we find ourselves confronted with an evil war, the sure elimination of which may be possible only by means of armed intervention.

I would prefer to embrace the position that condemns all violence. The Christian position of pacifism stands as a challenge to every generation of believers. But the atrocities being committed in Bosnia/Herzegovina challenge us, too. What is the morally correct thing to do?

We know that the intervention of armed international forces in the conflict amounts to answering violence with violence, while by no means guaranteeing that innocent people will not perish. Continued opposition to such intervention, however, remains virtually certain to condemn further innocent people to death—or to survival on brutal terms. Again, what are we to do?

I pose another question. Are we, as a religious and moral institution, to stand by and lend tacit support to a UN-sponsored arms embargo that, while even-handed on its face, has proven one-sided in effect? Can a policy which was clearly intended to diminish casualties—but which has served instead to foster the commission of atrocities and thereby expand the scope of suffering—be sustained?

A fundamental question now confronts the world community: Are we at a moment in history when humanitarian intervention by force into sovereign nations becomes a legitimate role of the United Nations? And if so, what are the criteria to be used in determining when and how such interventions occur, whether in the Balkans or elsewhere?

I pray fervently that peace negotiations will succeed. But if they fail, I do not want to issue another statement that simply deplores once again what is happening in the Balkans. That is simply just not enough.

Instead, I issue an urgent call to my religious counterparts to join me in a serious re-examination of this issue so that we might determine what God wills us to do on the European continent. Whatever shape that takes, I believe it will require that we take a firm public stand on these painful events.

Let me assure all the household of the Episcopal Church that I am engaged in this issue and seeking every means at my disposal to promote the cause of peace in this deeply troubled area of the world.

Statement on President Clinton's peace initiatives in Ireland and Bosnia, December 4, 1995

I want to congratulate President Clinton for the risks he is taking for peace in Ireland and Bosnia. When he addressed the huge and enormously appreciative crowd in Belfast, he commended the Irish people's yearning for peace by invoking Scripture when he said "blessed are the peacemakers."

The President, too, has taken on the noble cause of peacemaking. I can think of no greater mantle for the President of the United States to wear than that of peacemaker. It brings honor to him and to the United States. And it is my prayer that such will be his legacy. Our country has been searching for its proper role in the wake of the end of the cold war and I think the President has discovered part of that role.

I am among those who begged the President to take steps to end the atrocities in Bosnia. He has now done that with determination and high purpose. My gratitude to him is for lifting up moral values in shaping his policy in Bosnia and Ireland. While he points to US interests, it is the moral part of his argument that is compelling and right.

There will be those who oppose the use of troops in a conflict overseas. And I, too, have been in that position for a long time. The President has proven himself right in keeping troops out of Bosnia until a peace agreement has been reached. Now it is worth the risk for US troops to maintain and implement a peace already made. The world could not bear any longer to allow the atrocities of that conflict to continue. I am so relieved to see the end of that repugnant practice known as ethnic cleansing.

I am also relieved that our troops are not being sent into Bosnia to engage in combat, but rather are there to engage in peacemaking. Soldiers cannot ultimately do the hard work of reconciliation and healing. But they can hold the promise of

establishing the conditions in which a deep and enduring reconciliation can be pursued. Part of any genuine peacemaking
must also include the eventual removal of such forces where
the parties to the conflict maintain the peace from within their
hearts and through their inner resolve.

I pray for the day when all countries, including our own,
will lay down their arms, a day when violent conflict will be
obsolete. But that day is not yet at hand. And the path our President has chosen is courageous and moral and deserving of our
support. I ask that we remember him in prayer along with those
troops who go to Bosnia for the cause of peace.

Ireland

**The above statement was issued shortly after President
Clinton made his historic visit to Ireland. One of Browning's
staff was included in Clinton's delegation. Over the years,
Browning carried on a dialogue with the Primate of the
Church of Ireland about the civil unrest in Northern Ireland.
In January, 1994, they issued a joint statement calling for
fair employment and investment in Northern Ireland which
resolved a long standing dispute between the Episcopal
Church and its Irish partner. The dispute had been over the
MacBride Principles, a series of anti-discrimination
standards for US companies, which General Convention
adopted in 1988.**

Russia

**The remarkable dismantling of the Berlin Wall and the
breakup of the Soviet Union shortly afterwards are defining moments of the 20th century. Browning made a visit to
Russia just prior to the beginning of those events.**

Reflections from Russia: in *The Episcopalian*, September 1989

As I write this I am in the final day of three weeks in the Soviet Union. Patti and I came here in mid-July for the meeting of the Central Committee of the World Council of Churches. Then, as guests of the Russian Orthodox Church, we visited Christian sisters and brothers in the Ukraine, Georgia, Armenia, and Latvia.

A great deal happened in the days we traveled around this vast land. We met many people I will never forget—people I will remember when I read about the slow recovery from the devastating earthquake in Armenia, or about the ethnic struggles in various parts of this Union, or the new days of hope and promise for this nation. Though I will be mining the treasures of this experience for quite some time, I do have some preliminary impressions to share.

During the past decades when most churches were closed, the believers continued as a silent worshiping community, deep in prayer and growing in the faith. The experience of God's people has been that perseverance in the face of adversity can lead to ever more faithful witness. This is not always the case. Seeds scattered on infertile ground can wither. Yet this has not happened in the Soviet Union. Their desert experience has prepared the church to respond to this new moment in history.

Now the churches are reopening—and they are filled with people. We saw a worshiping community deeply committed to the saints of the past and nurtured in the teaching and tradition of the fathers. On the several occasions that we took part in the liturgy, we were all overwhelmed with the presence of the holy.

My second impression concerns the effects of *perestroika* on the church. I believe there is a growing recognition on the part of the state that it needs the church, that the church helps to set the foundation and restore the values that will bring well-being to the society.

This is also true at home. I remind myself that partnership with the state does not remove from the church the prophetic nature of its ministry, especially around justice and peace issues. We must also remind ourselves, as well as our governments, that it is God who gives the peace that passes all understanding.

The reopening of churches after decades of repression has placed a tremendous challenge before the church to provide an adequate number of clergy and train them to equip the laity to contribute to the changing society. The society is also coping with all of the logistical problems of reopening church buildings. They need our prayers.

My third impression has to do with the power of the Orthodox church as a family of churches, and the opportunity they have to bring witness to the world of God's redeeming love as they live together as a very diverse family. The Orthodox Church in the Soviet Union has a tremendous challenge to discover how they can model unity in diversity in the midst of a pluralistic society marked by ethnic and cultural differences. They will need to honor their own pluralism, determine the needs of each part of the church, and how the family of the church can reach out to meet those needs. They will need to discover the special hurts and wounds of one part of the church to which the whole family will respond.

That all sounds very familiar. As we look at our own church, the diversity of cultural and ethnic backgrounds, of economic conditions, of opinions on a whole range of theological, social and political issues provide us with one of our greatest challenges. That is, how can we enable that diversity to be honored with integrity, such that each part might respect the others, so that the whole church will be strengthened to serve the world for which Christ died?

In Riga, Latvia, I was interviewed by a reporter from TASS, the Soviet news agency. Among her questions was one about President Bush. I shared with the reporter that he is an

Episcopalian, a committed churchman, a man of prayer and an open and caring person. She then asked my opinion of Mr. Gorbachev. I said that I believed he was a man of vision and that he had done much to enhance the image of the Soviet Union in the minds and hearts of the American people.

I told her that what I hear from both men is that there is something more than national security. There is mutual security, global security. We are coming out of a period when, given the tension between our two nations, national security was an obsession with both of us, causing serious problems throughout the world, as well as within our two nations. I said it is my great hope that we are also coming into a period when the question will not be, "What is in my best interest?" but rather, "What is in the best interest of all God's people?"

Setting my watch back eight hours as we slip through several time zones on the way home reminds me that time is relative. What matters is God's time. My sense is that the Church is in a kairos time, both in the Soviet Union and in the United States. We can be thankful for our national leaders. We can be thankful that, as never before, we are called by God to preach the gospel of hope, the hope that undergirds the search for justice and the quest for peace.

THE PACIFIC
Hawaii

The Presiding Bishop made his official visitation to his former diocese in October, 1993, the 100th anniversary year of the overthrow of the Hawaiian monarchy by the United States government.

Sermon to Hawaii's diocesan convention at St. Michael and All Angels', Lihue, Kauai, October 22, 1993

What happened 100 years ago in these islands with the overthrow of a legitimate and sovereign government is a memory that challenges us powerfully today, the whole church, the whole country, not just this diocese or state. I want to affirm that it is the place of this Church to be in solidarity with our Hawaiian sisters and brothers, within and without the Church, and to acknowledge their right to seek justice and dignity of personhood, which is a trust the monarchy gave us in establishing this church in these islands. It is a trust we must honor.

Further, we all need to participate with our collective memories in listening and discerning what justice requires and what sovereignty means 100 years later. We recall the memories of the past to see God's justice for the future, justice that embraces the social, political and economic needs of the original peoples of these islands . . .

While supporting equality through civil laws, the Church seeks also understanding and reconciliation through love so that justice may be done. So simple and yet so hard. In the hundred and more years of the Church's witness in these islands, grace has intertwined with sin more than once. It was ever thus in human affairs, and life here is no exception to that unhappy rule . . . So when, at last, we see a wrong, we must strive to right it. If it is our wrong, we must repent of it. May all of us gathered here strive to show forth God's glory in the world so that everyone who sees us will know . . . that we proclaimed God's justice for these times.

IV
PEACEMAKING

NUCLEAR WEAPONS

The threat of nuclear war loomed large over the world when Bishop Browning began his term as Presiding Bishop. With the collapse of the Soviet Union tensions lessened. Concerned over the continuing production of these weapons, and moved by his conscience, Browning joined others in 1995 and issued an apology for the bombs used in Hiroshima and Nagasaki. This statement coincided with another issued a year later by the Anglican Church in Japan which apologized for the complicity of the church in the war waged by Japan.

Acceptance Speech, General Convention, September 1985

I have sent to Archbishop Paul Reeves, Primate of New Zealand, greetings and support of his witness for a nuclear free Pacific. I join in the support of those peoples, communities, and nations in the Pacific basin, especially our Anglican brothers and sisters in New Zealand who in political, economic, and moral self-determination decide against their own participation in any nuclear arms race, in the testing of nuclear weapons, nuclear waste disposal or any nuclear power development.

My position on the nuclear arms race is well known in my

diocese. A visit to the memorial in Hiroshima several years ago did much to awaken a sleeping conscience. I said then, and I re-affirm now, that I believe the production, testing, and deployment of nuclear, chemical and biological weapons to be incompat-ible with the Gospel of Jesus Christ.

You may recall the agnostic's remark at the time of Pope John 23rd's death. He said of John—"His life has made my unbelief uncomfortable." Just maybe part of our role is making uncomfortable those whose answers we hear being given in the name of security, by bringing a different kind of hope that will lift the "mushroom cloud" from God's creation.

Installation address, January 11, 1986

It is because we seek the face of Christ in all humanity that I am called to challenge anything that desecrates the creation and denigrates personhood. The concept of a nuclear holocaust is a sacrilege that destroys the very image of God.

Letter signed by Browning and others on the fiftieth anniversary of the atomic bombings of Hiroshima and Nagasaki, June 21, 1995

The image of the atomic mushroom cloud is etched forever in human memory as we commemorate the fiftieth anniversary of the bombings of Hiroshima and Nagasaki. We, the under-signed citizens of the United States, express our profound sorrow to the Japanese people as we recall the suffering and death left in the wake of the destruction of the two cities. On behalf of those peace-loving people of our country who grieve over the decision of our government to drop the bombs and the unimag-inable pain inflicted upon the families and survivors of the doomed cities, we extend a heartfelt apology. We are deeply sorry for the agony caused by these actions, and we ask for your forgiveness.

This apology does not ignore the atrocities committed by Japanese forces in their march across Asia, nor does it forget the suffering and death of those in the occupied countries, among the Allies, and those in the armed forces. But we reject mass killing and obliteration bombings as acceptable policies then or now. Means and ends are inextricably related, as the seed is to the tree. We feel it necessary to acknowledge and atone for the decision of our nation to introduce the use of atomic weapons and for the subsequent nuclear arms race which still hangs over the head of civilization.

In the fifty years since the war ended, many in the United States and Japan have worked tirelessly to promote reconciliation and friendship between our two peoples. With our signatures below, we solemnly pledge to continue these efforts. We promise to work with our Japanese friends and with others around the world for universal disarmament and the creation of a global culture of peace.

WAR

Sermon given at Washington Cathedral on the 45th anniversary of the bombing of Pearl Harbor

Then the wolf shall live with the sheep, and the leopard lie down with the kid; and the calf and the young lion shall grow up together, and a little child shall lead them . . . Isaiah 11:6

Today is the 7th day of December. It is, in the liturgical calendar, the Second Sunday of Advent. However, it also marks the anniversary of a dramatic event in the life of our country, "a day that will live in infamy." It was on this day 45 years ago that a nation which the United States had once considered a friend unleashed its warplanes on Pearl Harbor, sinking or damaging 19 ships and killing over 3,000 servicemen. A Sunday morning 45 years ago.

Japan had enjoyed a special relationship with the United States since Commodore Perry had opened its ports to the West. A country which had, in a December of 20 years earlier, joined with us in signing a Four-Power Treaty pledging to limit naval power and to respect each other's rights in the Pacific. And this same nation is today one of our major trading partners and is regarded by most Americans as one of our closest friends and allies in the world.

And yet, for a short time, Japan and the United States were mortal enemies bent on the "wholesale destruction by fire and sword" of each other's land and people.

So today, this important anniversary day in December, is a good time to reflect upon how easily friends become enemies . . . and then become friends again. It takes but a fraction of a lifetime for a relationship to turn against itself, then turn again, no matter how stolidly adversaries are set against each other, no matter how loudly proclaimed the vows of friendship, no matter how much passes between them . . .

It is in the nature of humankind to struggle with one's neighbor. And it is the nature of humankind to live in peace.

These opposing natures suffer an uneasy balance in all of us. Too often is the balance tipped, if only for a short while, towards struggle. And yet, we see that the balance is always restored—often at great cost—but an equilibrium of tolerance is the end of all struggles. Never mind the explosiveness of the issues which brought on the struggle in the first place.

It is John the Baptist who lies across our approach to the Feast of the Prince of Peace. It is John who stands in the wilderness, preparing the way of the Lord with radical "repentance." Repentance is the Hebrew word which implies a turning around, changing direction. In the preaching of John, repentance was the resolution not to repeat the action. Repentance was a transformation, a dying and rebirth, symbolized in the baptismal immersion in the waters of the Jordan River . . .

Repentance is the radical action that leads to peace. It is repentance that gives nations, races, neighbors the reflective pause to consider and reach out to that part of their nature that yearns for peace . . .

This is the great dream, it is the dream of the prophets who call us to maintain our hope with fortitude. It is the dream of the wolf living with the sheep which we hear in Isaiah. It is the vision of Paul in the letter to the Romans. He writes not of peace coming down from heaven but rather of peace coming about within the human community, completing what Jesus had begun. "Love your neighbor as yourself." This is the second great commandment. It is the commandment of peace through justice. No fuzzy dreams or romantic imaginings. The price of peace is clear: the ruthless will be struck down, the wicked will be slain. Evil will be overcome by a little child. The paradox is that injustice and oppression will not be overcome with the clash of armaments but by the word of the Lord incarnate . . .

It is worth noting that, though 1986 has been dubbed "The International Year of Peace" by the United Nations, more than 40 countries are officially at war. The number of global armed conflicts, often internal, has been pegged at well over 100. Current events have made us keenly aware that the global arms trade is a highly profitable business: Governments selling arms are paid over $30 billion a year for the latest variations; and military budgets of nations around the world now add up to well over $800 billion, an amount far exceeding the combined gross national product of the developing world. Need I draw attention to the moral implications of these facts?

How much better humanity would be if we kept in check that part of our natures which would give us over to violent struggle. How much better if we could ignore the counsel of those voices which urge us to violence, to seek revenge, to exact retribution, to protect honor. If we give in, let us give in to the side of our nature which presses us toward the inevitable: Peace.